AF477023

All
about
Individual
Medley

'Swimming Hall of Fame' Bookshelf

All about Individual Medley

All Four Strokes

Deryk Snelling
1974 Canadian Olympic Coach

William Luscombe

First published in Great Britain by
William Luscombe Publisher Ltd
The Mitchell Beazley Group
Artists House
14 Manette Street
London W1V 5LB

© 1975 Deryk Snelling

ISBN 0 86002 016 9

Text set in 11/12½ pt. Monotype Plantin, printed by letterpress,
and bound in Great Britain at The Pitman Press, Bath

Contents

Illustrations

There are also 64 drawings in the text

Acknowledgements

I should like to extend my thanks and appreciation to all the people who have helped me with the research involved in putting this book together, in particular:

Tor Bengtson
Pat Besford
Buck Dawson
Roy Grimshaw
John P. Hussey
Francois Oppenheim
Luigi Saini
Steven C. Saur
Nick Thierry

Foreword

by James E. Counsilman

Deryk Snelling's ability as a coach can best be judged by looking at the international swimmers he has coached, both in England and in Canada.

He has been Head Coach of the Canadian Dolphin Swim Club of Vancouver for the past six years. But his experience as both competitor and coach extends over many years.

He was a British National swimmer and English Champion prior to entering the British Army as a physical training instructor. In 1962 he was appointed Head Coach of the Southampton Swimming Club in England where he established a strong squad which included many Internationals. During this time his club were National Team Champions and three of his swimmers—Alan Kimber, Ray Terrell and Nigel Kemp were dominating the British individual medley scene. In fact his programme was responsible for Terrell being selected as the youngest-ever English International at the age of thirteen. He placed such swimmers as Kimber, Terrell and David Haller on European and Olympic teams. He has encouraged many of his former swimmers to take up coaching. Among his proudest moments were seeing David Haller, now head coach of Southampton Swimming Club, and his successor, named British Coach of the Year for the past three years.

His recent successes are impressive. He was appointed Head Coach of the Canadian Dolphin Swim Club in November 1967. Since his arrival in Canada, the Dolphins have been Canadian National Team Champions every year. His swimmers have set literally hundreds of Canadian records during that time.

His swimmers have won gold, silver and bronze medals at the major Games, including Commonwealth, Pan American,

Olympic and World Aquatic Games. He has placed competitors on teams for the past three Olympic Games. But his finest achievement in this field must be in placing no less than fourteen of his swimmers on the 1972 Canadian Olympic team for Munich. Five of his girls filled all six individual medley places, Leslie Cliff 'doubling' in the 200 and 400 metres events. In the same year, a visiting Welshman, Roland Jones, trained with the club and gained a place in the British Olympic Team in the 400 metres individual medley.

He has also been very active personally at the national level. He was Canadian Team coach for the Pan American Games in 1971, the 1972 Olympic Games, the First World Aquatic Championships in Belgrade in 1973, and for the 1974 Commonwealth Games in Christchurch, New Zealand. More recently he has been named Canadian Head Swimming Coach for both the 1975 World Aquatic Championships and the 1976 Olympic Games. His travels as Head Coach of Canadian touring teams have taken him to many places, including Brazil, Australia and to several United States Nationals where his Canadian Dolphin swimmers have made an impressive record.

James E Counsilman

Preface

The International Swimming Hall of Fame has undertaken a series of books isolating various strokes so that a swimmer specializing in a certain stroke or event may read all about that event in one source. In effect, this means the dryland exercises and the water training, as well as the starts, turns, and water mechanics peculiar to any stroke can be found without sorting it out from the general information that applies to all swimming. Any one of the books in this series may be purchased individually or as part of the collection, a virtual thesaurus of competitive swimming departmentalized by individual strokes.

In such a series there are, of course, books on each of the four strokes: breaststroke, backstroke, butterfly and crawl. The latter is further broken down into sprint crawl and distance freestyle. It is also appropriate and quite logical, we think, that there be a separate book on individual medley, and that this be the first book published in this new series. Teddy Stickles, the first man under five minutes for the 400 metre Individual Medley and the first under two minutes for the 200 yard I.M., properly labelled I.M. "the 5th stroke" since many swimmers now train for it as their primary event.

Deryk Snelling, the dynamic coach of the Vancouver Dolphins, is the logical man to write such a book, not only because he has produced great I.M. swimmers but because his philosophy of training breeds I.M.'rs. We are fortunate that this book not only tells us all about coaching, training and stroking an I.M. swimmer and an I.M. programme, but it also gives us many insights into this remarkable British and Canadian coach. In this book are some new ideas and reinforcement of old ideas that will help any coach or swimmer regardless of stroke or distance. As the late, great Matt Mann often proclaimed: 'A book is worth reading if I learn one new idea or rediscover an old idea I had forgotten'. Deryk Snelling's *All About Individual Medley* showed me several new approaches to training and reinforced my belief and therefore my confidence in several ideas of my own. I hope every swim buff reads his books and enjoys the experience, as I have.

BUCK DAWSON,
Executive Director
International Swimming
Hall of Fame.

Florida,
United States.

Introduction

Although much has been written about the separate strokes that make up the individual medley, there is little information available on the event as a whole. In this book I have attempted to 'fill the gap' by providing a comprehensive insight into the psychology and training of individual medley competitors. I have aimed to present my ideas from a practical point of view and most of the material is based on my own experience as a coach.

Individual Medley is an event which combines all four competitive strokes—butterfly, backcrawl, breaststroke and freestyle—which are swum over an equal distance. The strokes are put together in the above order. The last stroke, freestyle, is defined as any stroke apart from the three already included. In top-class competition this is always front crawl, being the fastest stroke.

There are now two racing distances for men and women that are generally recognized, 200 metres and 400 metres (200 yards and 400 yards short-course). In the 200 metres 50 metres of each stroke is swum and 100 metres of each stroke is swum in the 400 metres event. Both these distances have been included in the Olympic Games and hold recognized World Records. But as yet these events have not been permanently established as Olympic events. For instance, the 200 metres which has been swum at the past two Olympics, has been deleted from the programme of the 1976 Olympic Games in order to cut down on the number of events. But fortunately for all swimming enthusiasts the inaugural World Aquatic Championships in Belgrade did include both Individual Medley distances in the full programme of events. And the tremendous I.M. performances, particularly in the women's events where the two world records were completely 're-written', proved to be one of the sensations of the Championships.

It is important that swimming's unique and continuous all-round event be held in both Olympic and International competition over the 200 and 400 distances. If the decathlon winner in athletics (track and field) is declared the best all-round athlete, there is an equally good argument for declaring the Individual Medley winner (particularly a double I.M. winner) the all-round swimming champion.

Vancouver,
British Columbia,
Canada.

History of the Individual Medley

So how did it all start, this desire to put it all together and win the individual medley? The ancient Greeks had no Olympic swimming *per se*, but they did have a military pentathlon that scored various warrior skills in a sporting contest. The modern (military) pentathlon requires that the warrior (a hypothetical courier) run, swim, fence, shoot and ride. This event presents swimming (300 metres across a mythical river) as part of a series of all-round skill challenges.

Around the turn of the century (September 1901), L. deB Handley, later a famous swimming coach, author and American Hall of Famer, was competing for the Knickerbocker and the N.Y. Athletic Clubs in an omnibus event that was simply called 'The Medley.' Each athlete would walk, run, horseback-ride, bicycle, row and swim a quarter mile of each for a tough and talent-demanding mile and one half race. Handley's two cups as World Record Holder (15:42) and U.S. National Champion are now on display at the Swimming Hall of Fame in Fort Lauderdale, Florida.

Throughout its early history (1840 to 1920), swimming was so busy evolving new strokes in trying to ascertain the fastest way a human could get through the water that almost all races were freestyle. Galas and water shows usually included demonstrations of these strokes progressing from breaststroke through sidestroke, English single overarm, double overarm, trudgen and various forms of crawl including Australian, opposite action armstroke and legkick (two beat) up through four, six, eight and even ten leg-beat American crawl strokes. The original, breaststroke, hung in there from the first Olympics. Back breaststroke (inverted) began in 1900 and back crawl began with the 1912 Games. Butterfly with the fishtail kick was finally accepted at the 1956 Games, although butterfly arms as part of the breaststroke (frogkick) was prominent as early as the 1936 Games. The last Olympic freestyle winner using sidestroke was Emil Rausch of Germany in the 1904 Games at St. Louis. Soon after 1904 the sidestroke disappeared as a competitive stroke. For some reason unknown to the author it has never returned as part of the individual medley.

The first individual medley champion was not a man, but a woman . . . an English woman, Hilda James, of Liverpool who won the first I.M. in the U.S. Nationals in 1922. It was more than two years before the men began swimming the I.M. as a national or international event.

Prior to 1953 the individual medley was three-stroke (150 yards or metres and 300 yards or metres), more often yards than metres and more often American than world-wide, but nevertheless a world-rated world record event accepted in the U.S. Nationals (A.A.U. and College) since 1925.

The individual medley was not the first all-round event accepted in swimming, however. That honour goes to the Germans for the 'Mehr Kampf', a several event championships, swimming underwater (50 metres), over water (100 metres) and six dives. A swimmer would compete in the three events separately as individual races with a short rest between. The 'Mehr Kampf' (high point trophy) was presented to the overall winner, in this German event popular until the middle 1930's.

In the United States, the all-round event preceeding the individual medley for men was the swimming pentathlon where the first American Nationals in 1923 ended in a tie between the great Illinois Athletic Club swimmers Johnny Weissmuller and Stubby Kruger. Weissmuller's accomplishments as the world's premier freestyler plus his pentathlon win may qualify him for the mythical crown as the 'World's All-Time Greatest All-round Swimmer.'

Kruger was a world record holding backstroker and a freestyle sprinter who went on to become the world's premier water show comedy diver and still later a Hollywood stuntman.

Kruger's last role before his death was stand-in for Spencer Tracy in swimmer Ernest Hemingway's *Old Man and the Sea*. One of Stubby's most notorious distinctions was that his world record (400 metres backstroke) was the only current men's record ever broken by a woman (Sybil Bauer in Bermuda, October 7, 1922).

The pentathlon consisted of five events and is described in the 1924 A.A.U. Athletic Almanac and Swimming Rules as follows:

Pentathlon

(a) The Pentathlon consists of 100 yards any style except breast and back. 100 yards backstroke, 100 yards breaststroke, 500 yards any style and the 50 yard life saving race, to be contested in the order named.

(b) The 50 yard life saving race is to consist of a 25 yard swim to the subject and a 25 yard tow using any hold. The subject's face and mouth must be kept above the water subject to the decision of the judges. The subject is to be the same for each competitor. Three judges are to be named by the Referee and the three judges shall agree upon the holds and the nature of the contest. Each contestant shall swim separately and have his time taken. If a turn is required, the competitor must touch the wall above the water with one hand.

(c) The clerk of course shall draw the contestants before each event and they shall be assigned to lanes or compete in the order in which they have been drawn.

(d) Each competitor must compete in every one of the five events. The contest will be decided on points according to the place number of the contestants in each race which shall be added, and the one with the lowest total shall be declared the winner. Should a competitor be disqualified he shall be assigned to the last place in the contest. In the event of a tie, the competitors need not compete again. If two or more obtain the same result, those so tieing receive the same points and the next man receives a point corresponding to the position in which he finishes relative to all other competitors. An interval of at least five minutes shall be allowed between events.

The pentathlon lasted only four years as a national event, then faded as the I.M. came on. Stubby Kruger the first pentathlon winner (with Weissmuller) was also the U.S.A.'s first 300 I.M. National Champion in the 1924 Nationals. Walter Laufer, high point winner at the 1926 U.S. Nationals (over Weissmuller) and the only living man who won both the pentathlon (1926) and the I.M. (1926 and 1928) has this to say in comparing the early days of these two events:

'Looking back nearly fifty years to my years of active competition in A.A.U. National Swimming Championships, my sharpest recollections concern the versatility, stamina and endurance required in the pentathlon event. This demanding event was discontinued after 1926, and relatively few swimmers (only four or five) elected to compete during the last few years the event was held. This race involved 100-yard sprints in backstroke, breaststroke and freestyle followed by a 500-yard freestyle leg and finally five dives (two compulsory and three elective). Each event was followed by a five-minute rest period.

'In degree of difficulty, I would rate the three-stroke individual medley of the middle 1920's as more difficult than any one-stroke event because of the "opposing" strokes involved. Certainly, today's four-stroke medley which includes the butterfly is even more difficult. However, I would rate the pentathlon as even more difficult than either of the medley races because of the greater distance involved and the added skills required by the diving event.

'My own personal strategy in both the individual medley and the pentathlon races was to swim the fastest time among my competitors in the backstroke and freestyle legs. I would usually have to settle for second or third best in the breaststroke leg. Being an old "river swimmer", I was raised on distance swimming and always managed to do well in the

500-yard freestyle leg. Surprisingly, I've always looked upon diving as fun; and during the years that I "worked" at competitive swimming, I considered diving as diversion and recreation. As a result of this, my timing, practice and knowledge of diving paid off in the pentathlon, and I usually did quite well in this last of the five component events.

'In training for the two races I would, of course, swim longer distances in preparation for the pentathlon. Beyond swimming for time in the sprints, I would swim 500 yards for time, then an extra 100 yards to build stamina for the distance event. Additionally, I would spend time sharpening my diving skill and timing. In addition to the compulsory front (swan) and back dives, I would usually do a full twist, a one-and-a-half twist and a half-gainer.

'I would have to say that I still take a special pride in being the record holder in the pentathlon, since I won the event the last year it was held. Including the diverse elements of sprint strokes, distance and diving, I feel that the pentathlon provided the best measure of all-round aquatic ability at that time. But since we no longer compete in pentathlon I would have to defer to the four-stroke 400 metre individual medley being the best test of the all-round swim champion today.'

Walter Laufer's reflections—and also a verbal recollection from Johnny Weissmuller—indicate that the pentathlon included diving, contrary to the rules of the *AAU Handbook*. 'In fact,' says Weissmuller, 'It was in diving that Stubby Kruger caught up and tied with me.'

Perhaps the most accomplished all-round athlete to go into swimming and to win the U.S. Nationals in individual medley (seven times) is Buster Crabbe. Crabbe was a five-sport star at Honolulu's famous Panahou School in football, basketball, baseball, athletics (track) and swimming before concentrating on swimming while studying law at the University of Southern California. Crabbe, who later became a movie athlete as Flash Gordon, Buck Rogers, Billy the Kid and Tarzan (quite an individual medley on film!) has this to say about his recollections of swimming the I.M.:

'Actually I backed into the event. I could always swim the back and breast fairly well although I was a middle distance and distance freestyler, which gave me the endurance. The date was the spring of '27 and a dual meet was arranged between Panahou H.S., of which I was captain, and the University of Hawaii with Sam Kahanamoku as captain. It was a tough dual for us . . . we were younger and needed all the points we could get so I decided to enter the 150 yards I.M. hoping to pick up a point. I swam away with the thing and it started me thinking. The National Outdoors were scheduled for the new Memorial Natatorium in Honolulu that summer of '27 and all the big boys were due to compete . . . Weissmuller, Laufer, Wyatt, Kojac, Spence—the lot, so over and above the 440, 880 and mile, I trained as well for the 300 I.M. This training included entering breast and back races in dual meets and in the Hawaiian Championships that June. Warren Kealoha barely beat me in the 100 metres back and believe it or not, I won the breaststroke which really floored Dad Center. The only time I was ever beaten in the Medley was the summer of 1927 when I ran a close second to Walter Spence. Kojac was third and Laufer fourth. From then until the Games of 1932 I held all the medley records—150 yards, 300 yards and 300 metres. Unfortunately there was no I.M. in the Games. As my forte was distance, the longer the I.M. the better for me.'

Swimming's Medley Family would have to be the Spence brothers—Walter, Leonard and Wallace—South American Indians from the then British Guiana. This trio not only was the only brother act ever to hold a world record for the medley relay (300 yards), but each won the U.S. Nationals in the individual medley (Walter in 1925, 26, 27 and 29, brother Wallace in 1933 and Leonard in 1934 and 1935). Walter and Leonard also won repeated U.S. breaststroke titles. They represented Bermuda in one Olympic Games and Canada in another. Walter was selected U.S. College Swimmer of the Year in 1935 aged thirty-five with times of 23.1 (50 yards), 51.6 (100 yards) and 2:11.6 (220 yards). As if their records were not enough, all three Spence brothers could roll up their pants legs at press conferences and show piranha bites on their legs from their learn-to-swim days in the Demerara River. Even a modern age-group mother can't provide that kind of incentive to swim fast! Walter Spence was also 1925 winner of the pentathlon.

Eleanor Holm made three Olympic teams (1928, 1932 and 1936) in backstroke and later worked even harder in six shows a day as star of the Billy Rose (she married him) World's Fair Aquacades. She also won the U.S. Nationals nine consecutive times (five years) in the 300 I.M. and here tells of her regret that it was not then accepted as an Olympic event:

'Medley swimming required triple training periods. Each stroke needed concentration. To me it was a personal satisfaction to be a champion in all three strokes. In my day it was not an Olympic event, which made me unhappy, as I felt I could have won another gold medal. In my case, I could stay up with the lead-off breaststroke. The next leg, backstroke, which was by forte, I would get such a lead I had no trouble keeping it on the freestyle.'

No I.M. swimmer ever dominated the world for so long as Katherine Rawls. This tiny girl also won U.S. Nationals in three-metre springboard diving, all freestyle events (from 100 metres up through the mile) and in several combinations of breaststroke. Even the great U.S. women swimmers would try and wait to see what Katherine was entering before they would turn in their entry cards. Katherine Rawls stayed out of Eleanor Holm's backstroke races and after Katherine came on the scene, Eleanor stayed out of Katherine's private race, the individual medley. Rawls describes how she switched back and forth between conventional breaststroke and butter-fly-breaststroke in developing a specificity of training rest factor for maximum use of rested muscle combinations:

'It was my favourite event . . . and by far the least tiring because each change of stroke was a welcome relief to the muscles. Even now when I swim laps, the change of strokes is like a fresh start. However, when I swam the I.M., it consisted only of the three strokes . . . butterfly was considered just another style of breaststroke. We could even interchange at will. I generally swam the first lap butterfly, then switched over to the conventional breaststroke. During my competitive years, I managed to break most of the world records in the I.M. and it was unfortunate for me that this event was not included in the women's Olympic programme as that would have afforded me the best opportunity to win the illusive gold medal. The event was considered too strenuous for women— what a joke! I do not recall any particular difference in training for the I.M. because I was competing in all strokes anyway. However, since backstroke was my weakest, I never entered a Nationals in that stroke, not while my friend Eleanor was around. She was tough! Actually my workouts were never longer than a mile in total laps except during the times I would go out for the half mile or mile, then I would concentrate a little more on distance. Besides the swimming, I had to do an hour of diving practice each day. I practised every day, year round. There were no vacations or off-season breaks. In South Florida, only a hurricane was sufficient cause to skip practice!'

While Weissmuller remembers doing the dolphin kick as early as 1923, and while much experimenting was done with it in the 30's the butterfly arm stroke with dolphin kick was not accepted by FINA until 1953 after which the I.M. went from three to four strokes. 'Bumpy' Jones, the last three-stroke and the first American four-stroke world record holder, describes the problems in converting from three strokes to four strokes where two of the four were now new (breast without butterfly arms and the new butterfly with dolphin kick):

'The biggest problem was that they changed all the rules, and several times in a period of three or four years. The world's greatest individual medley swimmer, Joe Verdeur, and other butterfly-breaststrokers, such as Bob Brauner and Johnny Davies, were stripped of their stroke and their records by a totally new stroke and a throw-back to a long abandoned old stroke.

'Not only was the new butterfly a fourth stroke but bringing back the 1932 style breaststroke to replace the newer butterfly-breaststroke meant eliminating one stroke and learning two more. The men who made the transition had to move from excelling in three strokes to excellence in five strokes. Then they kept changing the breaststroke around with new rules each year.

'I was lucky. A great many swimmers found they could do some version of the new fly but they were not necessarily the same men who had been the world's best at the butterfly-breast. Added to this, I could not find one coach in the continental U.S.A. who still knew how to coach the orthodox breaststroke. I went to Sakamoto in Hawaii for the summer and learned the stroke. He trained me with one length under-water repeats and when I got back to Michigan that fall, I was the team breaststroker as well as the new I.M.-er and still participated in my old freestyle races. We swam the 1932 Japanese style of breaststroke which was all under-water in short course swimming except for a breath at the turns. This was a pretty tough oxygen problem in the third quarter of a tough four-stroke I.M. In the I.M., a few of us had barely adjusted to the new fly and the new breaststroke when they changed the breaststroke again, this time to a pre-1928 European surface stroke.

'By then I was an angry young man. My biggest problems were not the mechanics of adjusting to the new strokes, but in making myself acquiesce to the bureaucrats' field day of rule changes. I am still asking why they eliminated the beautiful butterfly breaststroke.

'In retrospect, I would have to say the biggest change between three- and four-stroke I.M. was and is that in four-stroke, a good breaststroker has an advantage enjoyed by no one of the three-stroke specialists in the old I.M. This is because the surface breaststroke is the slowest stroke and a very good breaststroker gets to start his freestyle sprint while the slower breaststroke swimmer is still struggling to finish his breaststroke third leg.'

The first long course 400 metre World Record Holder was Australia's Frank O'Neill in March 1953 (the Australian summer). The individual medley changed again and slowed temporarily in 1957 when the Europeans through FINA insisted on bringing breaststroke up to the surface of the water, but new Jestremski breaststroke techniques (he was another great I.M. swimmer) soon made up for lost time. Dick Roth (U.S.A.) was the first 400 metres I.M. Olympic Champion at Tokyo in 1964. Other individual medley 'four minute mile' type break-throughs have come: in 1954—Burwell Jones (U.S.A.)—first FINA four-stroke individual medley world record 400 metres in 5:29.0; 1959—Sylvia Ruuska (U.S.A.)—first woman under five minutes for 400 yards I.M. in 4:58.2; 1961—Ted Stickles (U.S.A.)—first under five minutes for 400 metres I.M. in 4:55.6—Stickles, the first person to consider himself primarily an individual medley swimmer, was also the first to swim 200 yards I.M. in under two minutes (1962); 1973—Gudrun Wegner (East Germany)—first woman under five minutes for the 400 metres I.M. in 4:57.51.

Ted Stickles, one of the really great I.M. swimmers, had serious elbow problems and lost his chance at an Olympic medal. He stresses the value of four-stroke swimming to avoid boredom and feels the individual medley was and is a natural development from four-stroke training and a natural challenge for swimmers who have built up a big mileage background as young swimmers. Says Stickles:

'I started as a backstroke swimmer. That was practically everything that I then swam. Within one year I got fed up with this swimming style and started to swim the others. I cannot swim a long time in one swimming style without becoming restless and therefore I swam them all.'

'The competition in individual medley swimming, according to my point of view, has come of age itself since 1964,' says George Haines, who has coached more I.M. champions than any other coach. 'Firstly,' says Haines, 'the 400 metres medley swimming was introduced in the 1964 Olympics.

Therefore more boys through the whole world took this competition more seriously after that date. It made the whole sport much more exciting. Secondly, we have better training methods which improve the I.M. each year on the same level as the other swimming styles are improved.'

Claudia Kolb says:

'After having been a breaststroker it was interesting to see if I could make it as an I.M.-er. The workouts were more varied—they offered me tremendous variety in practice. Before, if we were swimming a series such as 10 × 200's I would go the majority of them all breaststroke. As an I.M.-er I could choose what particular stroke I wanted to work on or go an I.M. or break them up i.e. 100 fly, 100 back. If I didn't feel particularly good one day swimming freestyle I always had three other strokes to choose from. In the early part of every season I did a tremendous amount of freestyle as George and I felt that it was the best overall conditioner.

'Training for the I.M. was more difficult than training for one particular stroke (other than distance free) because most often I trained with the distance swimmers. A tremendous amount of strength and stamina is needed to swim a 400 I.M. well. As for swimming the I.M. in competition it was always a challenge. I knew exactly how I wanted to swim each leg of the I.M. but I wasn't always able to swim it as planned.

'George and I spent a lot of time trying to relax the butterfly part of my I.M. We felt that the key to my swimming it well depended on whether or not I was relaxed at the end of the fly. No matter how fast I was going I had to convince myself that the fly felt easy. If it was easy and I was out ahead at the end of the fly then I knew that I would win.

'On backstroke (my weakest stroke) I would just try to stay even and float my legs because I knew that I needed them for breaststroke. Often I would open my backstroke turn to get more air. I never flipped from back to breast because it would cut short my breaststroke pull-down which is very important.

'I can't remember doing much else in breaststroke other than swimming as fast as I could because it was always a place for me to gain on my opponents. I would try to be far enough ahead at the end of the breaststroke so that I could start swimming freestyle while everyone else was still swimming breaststroke. You can gain a good amount of yardage that way.

'Of course the freestyle was swum as best I could because at that point there is nothing to save for. I loved to swim the I.M. more than anything else because it always seemed like more of a challenge than any other event.'

In trying to evaluate the greatest individual medley swimmer of all time, and therefore the greatest all-round swimmer of all time, a table (Chapter 14) comparing world records in 100 metres for each of the four strokes is added together and compared with elapsed time for the I.M. World Record Holder where the four-stroke 100's are continuous. By such a standard (world record comparison at the time) we find that Gary Hall and Gudrun Wegner emerge as the two who come closest and therefore *by this criteria* they should be rated the world's two greatest all-time, all-round swimmers.

If you have some other favourite from your era, don't give up! There are other criteria and, at best, it is difficult to compare swimmers of different eras. Donna De Varona, for example, held world '100' records in three out of four events that make up the four-stroke individual medley, which has to be some kind of record. And Katherine Rawls, back in the 1930's, held the world record nine years for the 300 I.M. She won thirteen U.S. National I.M. titles and in addition won every other event in the U.S. Nationals except backstroke (I.M. swimmer Eleanor Holm's speciality) and tower diving. Dick Roth had his appendix frozen before winning the 400 metres I.M. at the Tokyo Olympics. No man ever put it all together better to win the I.M. year after year than Dick, even though he was not a national or international champion in any of the four individual strokes as were his competitors— Roy Saari, Carl Robie, Charlie Hickcox and others just before, during and after Dick. Sylvia Ruuska, the first many-year champion and world record holder among four-stroke women I.M.-ers frequently coupled her I.M. wins with high point honours at the U.S. Nationals but all just before the I.M. was accepted as an Olympic event.

So be it in a sport where techniques, training and talent show no end to the record breaking. But the author cannot help but sympathize with the great all-round swimmers of the past: individual medley swimmers whose best event was not included in the Olympics. This book lists the complete records (Appendix) of these fine swimmers who swam their fast times before their time had come.

BUCK DAWSON

2
What makes an Individual Medley Swimmer?

The individual medley is the most demanding of all today's swimming events. It is the decathlon of swimming—the ultimate test of the all-round swimmer. It demands many qualities of a competitor: capacity for a heavy work-load, great speed, stamina, sense of pace and the finest all-round development of the four competitive strokes. Also the ability to turn and change smoothly from one stroke to another. I will enlarge on these points in later chapters.

As well as the physical side of things, attitude to this event is extremely important and must be properly developed before any respectable times can be recorded. But the swimmer who wants to excel in this event is usually a satisfying pupil to coach. Every coach likes to feel that his pool time is being used to full advantage. The programme for the individual medley swimmer must be completely comprehensive, both in distance swum and in variety of strokes. There is never one stroke, one isolated practice, kick, pull or drill that will be a waste of time. For it is without doubt that unless all four strokes are moving well success in the event will be difficult.

The individual medley swimmer must be a great worker, for in preparation twelve separate units must be worked on and developed fully. These are the four different leg-kicks, the four arm pulls and the four full strokes. At no time can a swimmer afford to work on one stroke at the expense of another. So often you will find swimmers working to improve their weak link, only to neglect one or more of their stronger strokes. Work on all strokes must take place simultaneously, so that the level of performance is maintained in the good strokes while working on the weaker ones.

By coaching individual medley as an event you automatically

provide yourself with an all-round programme. There is plenty of scope for variety, with the need to work on all four strokes and both sprints and long distance swimming. It is important to guard against boring workouts with today's drive towards so much yardage in practice—which must be repeated day after day and month after month if a swimmer is to become a champion.

When to concentrate on Individual Medley ?

The earlier a swimmer can start on the individual medley the better. A good prospect should be potentially good in all four strokes and they must first be learned to some degree of proficiency. What often happens is that a competitor will enter I.M. as an 'extra' event, because he has two or maybe three strong strokes. And in local competition he may do well. Now this is not a bad starting point. But what is often not understood is that the individual medley swimmer must SPECIALIZE and prepare and train specifically for the event if he is to achieve success at higher levels. This preparation should be just as individual as that of a 1,500 metres freestyle or a 100 metres butterfly competitor.

PACE is another factor which can take years to learn—that is the swimmer's OWN pace—and the confidence to use tactics to real advantage. This subject is discussed fully in a later chapter. There is some carry-over from single-stroke events, but there is no match for experience. So the sooner a potential individual medley swimmer can be introduced to the event the better.

Hard training should start when the swimmer himself shows a desire to train harder than for the normal programme. For the individual medley means four times more work than a one-stroke swimmer must put in. At this time self-motivation has arrived and from now on fairly hard training can be introduced. As a general rule this is somewhere between eleven and twelve years for girls and thirteen or fourteen years for boys. This seems to be the point where the swimmer really starts to understand himself and knows that he wants to be a successful competitive swimmer.

At this time he is mentally, physically and probably emotionally ready to go into a regular training programme. A swimmer can take a tremendous amount of work provided he is self-motivated.

Breaststroke is the Key

It is really difficult to state with conviction which is the most important stroke in individual medley competition. However, as freestyle dominates most training programmes, we can assume that this stroke is adequately taken care of. The question then arises as to how much time should be spent on the other three strokes. To me the key is the breaststroke. For the other three strokes seem to have a tremendous amount of carry-over: similar leg action in front and back crawl, similar arm-movement in front crawl and butterfly, etc. But the breaststroke has to be worked on quite separately, as there is very little carry-over either in technique or timing and co-ordination. The only real carry-over is in the conditioning gained from training for the other strokes.

It is very important to have good breaststroke. When swimming the breaststroke leg in an I.M. race it is psychologically important to feel that you are either gaining on the opposition—coming from behind and feeling good in that position—or at least knowing that you have the ability to retain any lead that you have. Another reason for having strong breaststroke can be demonstrated if we take the example of an 'off' day in competition. If he is not performing well on any of the strokes then even on an equal percentage drop-off on all four strokes a swimmer will lose considerably on the breaststroke leg, as this is the slowest stroke.

Which event first—the 200 or 400 I.M?

It is desirable to develop the distance side of training at an early age. For this reason both the 200 and 400 should be swum right from the start. Many coaches encourage the idea of starting with the 200 and building up later to the 400. This is not logical, as the young swimmer finds stamina easier to develop than strength, which is necessary for the speed of the 200 distance. Witness results at the First World Aquatic Championships in Belgrade, Yugoslavia—September 1973. A seventeen-year-old Hungarian boy, Andras Hargitay, won the 400 metres individual medley. Whereas the 'old timer', Gunnar Larsson of Sweden, won the 200 metres I.M. Larsson is twenty-two, mature for a swimmer.

3
Profile of Leslie Cliff: International Individual Medley Competitor and Olympic Silver Medallist

I have chosen to write about Leslie Cliff as she is the most successful individual medley swimmer to emerge from my programme so far. As I have shown in a later chapter, this programme is very much geared to the 'all round' approach and so individual medley swimmers are a natural 'by-product'.

I have known and coached Leslie for the past six years. When I first arrived at the Canadian Dolphin Swim Club she was one of the young swimmers, aged twelve, who was working out at the time. She was not outstanding in any way—in fact the first time I remember seeing her she was swimming free-style and had an extremely wild and thrashing stroke with very poor form. But she had a tremendous amount of drive and I believe this is something that was there right from the beginning—it has always been there, she has never lost that aggressive desire to challenge those she is swimming. Over the years she has become more controlled and paced in her idea of how much effort she can put into a practice and this has certainly helped in many ways. Basically, Leslie has always been personally motivated to work hard. And I think this basic concept of being a hard worker is something that is absolutely essential in an I.M. swimmer, because there is so much to be learned and practised to swim four good strokes.

The fact that Leslie's strokes were technically very poor was in fact a good thing for me, her coach. Because over the past six years I have been able to coach all strokes in the way that I think they should be developed and I have worked on the continuous process of improving techniques as Leslie's strength and ability have increased. If she had come to me with set ideas on the four strokes when I first started to work with

Leslie Cliff, silver medallist in the 400 metres individual medley at the Munich Olympics, receives the Order of Canada medal from Roland Michener, Governor General of Canada

Double double: team mates Leslie Cliff and Bruce Robertson with the silver medals they won at the 1972 Olympic Games. They are also both American short-course champions (1973)—Leslie in 200 yards individual medley and Bruce in 100 yards butterfly.

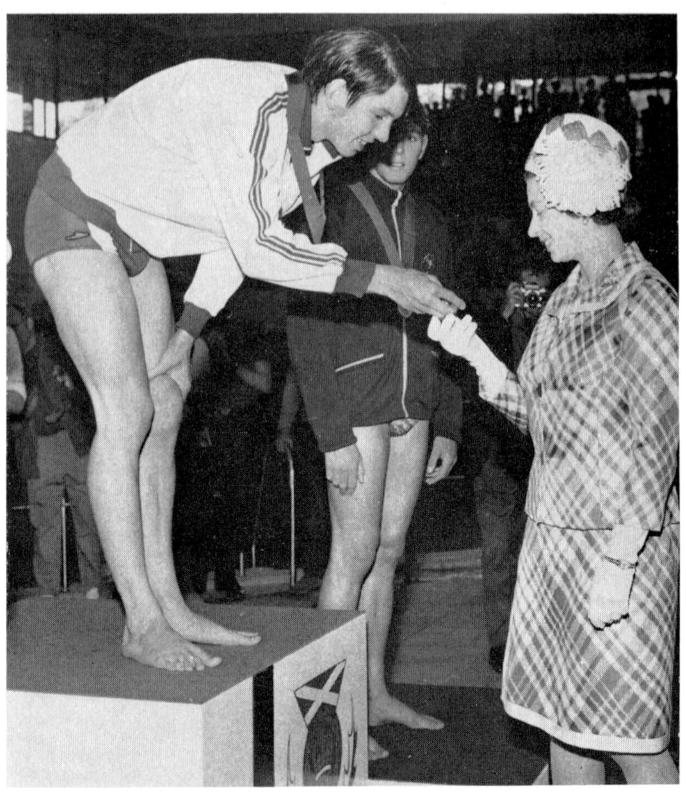

Breaststroke is one of the keys to coach Snelling's training programme. It bears little relationship to the other three strokes and so training has to be specific. Here Bill Mahony, Snelling's top breaststroker and winner of both the 100 and 200 metres breaststroke at the 1970 Commonwealth Games, is seen proudly handing his club pin to H.R.H. Queen Elizabeth II. He swam the breaststroke leg of the 4 × 100 medley relay in Munich, in which Canada won the bronze medal.

her, it may have been difficult for her to learn new techniques. As it was, I was able to develop all four strokes from the basics and build them up so that she could eventually put them together as an individual medley competitor.

Leslie has been an ideal swimmer to coach in the sense that we have developed her strokes over the years, knowing just where the strokes have come from, where they are now and exactly how we reached this point. And if a breakdown in stroke-form occurs, as often happens during heavy training periods when the emphasis is on hard work and conditioning rather than on form, we are able to go back through past experiences and know just how to rebuild the rhythm, the feel and the technique of her strokes.

Leslie has always been very willing to try new ideas. She applies herself fully to anything she does. For instance, if I am talking to a group of swimmers about technique during a practice and someone happens to be talking or moving around so that she cannot hear all that I'm saying, she becomes indignant and asks the swimmers to be quiet so that she can hear everything that I am saying. She is always actively positive. She feels that everything that we do in practice is valuable. This is really important, because every coach likes to feel that his swimmer has confidence in his teaching and co-operates with all he is trying to achieve. From this a very good relationship can develop. I am sure that a swimmer's positive attitude helps the coach to have a positive approach too. It works both ways. It cannot work properly if it is only one way. This is something that many swimmers overlook. The relationship that is built up over the years is an individual thing, and although a club swimming programme is basically team-orientated, it is imperative that time is spent counselling and talking to each swimmer individually. It is good to know that your advice is valued and taken seriously, just as you and the swimmer must know that she must do the job for and within herself once the race begins.

I find that in Leslie's case, she likes me to plan the whole of her programme and just give her a basic outline of what we are trying to achieve. She realizes that we have to be flexible, that we may change quite a bit and that we work on a long-term basis. I present the work and if Leslie understands it and is confident in it she just goes ahead. But if she has any doubt at all she asks to have it clarified. And then I know that she needs some explanation to give her the confidence necessary to go ahead. When it is straight in her mind she works on it as hard as she can, knowing that we've thought it through to the end of the season and somewhere what we are doing now fits into the whole pattern. She has the confidence in me and in herself to accept this idea. I find that I reinforce her confidence to a certain extent on a constant basis. But I never force any really hard ideas onto her. I find that just letting her work at her own pace is good for her and I known that if she wants my help at any time, whether it is at a meet or during a workout, she will make the first approach. This takes the pressure off us both. The feeling that a coach is forcing ideas onto his swimmer and over-shadowing every move she makes is common in age-group swimming, where a child seeks an absolute authority-figure. But it doesn't usually work with a mature or even a maturing swimmer who wants to 'do her thing'. This, I am sure, accounts for so much of the 'scrap heap' left after our age-group swim programmes.

Leslie has always been a keen and good competitor and thrives on difficult situations. I think this has contributed a lot to her ability to perform well in major competitions. For very often these meets are held under less-than-perfect conditions—we often have better conditions for our local meets than we do when we go to major competitions.

This conditioning and adapting to ever-changing situations really started back in 1969 when Leslie just qualified for our Canadian Championships. And that was the requisite to make our club team that was to tour Europe. This was a new adventure for us and we thought a good team-builder. The trip itself was pretty demanding. We left Vancouver for Amsterdam, then travelled to Geneva, Switzerland where we stayed for five days to compete three times against local clubs. We moved on into Germany and competed against the top West German team in Wuppertal, coached by Heinz Hoffman, West Germany's premier coach. Our next stop was London, where we trained at the new Crystal Palace Recreation Centre. Following our two-day stay in London, we travelled to Blackpool to compete in the English National Championships for six days. After the end-of-Championships party, which Leslie and all our swimmers attended, we had to get up early to travel to Montreal, which was another 3,000 mile trip. The next day we started to compete in the Canadian National Championships. At this time we were only just beginning to feel that as a club we could do well in these Championships. We had our four-day competition and Leslie performed very well. From there we travelled back east again, to Nova Scotia and the Canadian Summer Games. These were again held over a four-day period. By the time we reached the end of our trip we had been 'on the road' without proper workouts for something like forty days. During this period Leslie had competed 48 times and was still getting better, even on the last day of competition.

I believe that this type of demanding trip, with ever-changing locations and conditions and no regular routine, contributed a lot to Leslie's development at this time. It really made a tough competitor of her, and made her quite willing to take anything that came up, and still expect to swim well. This may not work for all swimmers but it is certainly a good 'omen' for individual medley swimmers. Coach Rosemary Dawson tells me the same thing happened with Donna De Varona and Dick Roth at the U.S. Nationals after a 28-day tour of Japan that she took them on in 1962.

I think that this toughness and ability to adapt to conditions has continued to carry through Leslie's swimming and has shaped her attitude towards the sport. It paid off very well in Cali, Colombia, where Leslie won the two individual medley events at the Pan-American Games, against Susie Attwood and some other great swimmers. I am sure that this was partly due to the fact that the conditions there were not ideal. Leslie was used to swimming her races under fairly tough conditions. Conditions that to some swimmers were poor, were pretty normal for Leslie. Our type of programme helps her. Also, at the Olympic Games in Munich, where transportation and accommodation problems upset some competitors, Leslie was not phased out in any way. Her tough mental attitude which she has built up helped her to come through to win the silver medal in the 400 metres I.M. and to make the finals in the 200 metres individual medley and the 200 metres backstroke. I strongly believe that this mental toughness is learned, not innate, and I think the lessons Leslie has learned have been pretty good condition reflexes for tough going.

Another example of toughness must be illustrated in the example of Donna-Marie Gurr, Canadian National backstroke swimmer. In 1970, prior to the Commonwealth Games trials, she developed a knee condition which could have put her out of training for several months. Instead, her doctor made a special light-weight cast so that she was able to continue on a modified training programme. The cast was temporarily removed for the trials, where she swam trailing her leg. She made the team and a few days later went on to win a silver medal in the 200 metres backstroke at the Games. The carry-over of this tough and determined attitude was demonstrated a year later in the Pan-American Games when a most remarkable thing happened during the final of the 200 metres backstroke, in which Donna was competing. The race took place outdoors in a floodlit pool and was tipped to be one of the great races as Sue Attwood and Barbie Darby (U.S.A.) were also competing. The race was close and tremendously fast at the approach to the 100 metre turn, when suddenly a city power cut took the lights out completely, and the girls were left floundering in pitch blackness, half-way through the most important race of the year for them. The re-swim later that evening really upset many of the competitors. But before she swam I said to Donna 'Take it easy, swimming this race twice is nowhere near as tough as dragging the cast around last year!' At that she laughed and went off with the other girls to rest. Two hours later she blasted the field to win the gold medal.

Leslie's Achievements to Date

Canadian Nationals, 1971

Won five individual Championships:

100 metres butterfly
200 metres butterfly
200 metres individual medley
400 metres individual medley
200 metres breaststroke

Pan American Games, 1971

Won three gold medals:

200 metres individual medley
400 metres individual medley
400 metres medley relay (fly)

two silver medals:

100 metres butterfly
400 metres freestyle relay

American Nationals, 1971

Won one silver medal: 400 metres individual medley
one bronze medal: 200 metres individual medley

Canadian Nationals, 1972

Won four individual Championships:

200 metres individual medley
400 metres individual medley
100 metres butterfly
800 metres freestyle

Olympic Games, 1972

Won one silver medal: 400 metres individual medley
Fifth: 200 metres individual medley
Eighth: 200 metres backstroke

American Nationals (short course), 1973

Won one gold medal:

200 yards individual medley
(American record)

one silver medal: 400 yards individual medley
one bronze medal: 200 yards backstroke

Canadian Nationals, 1973

Won four individual Champion- ships:	200 metres freestyle 800 metres freestyle 200 metres individual medley 400 metres individual medley

Awards

British Columbian Junior Athlete, 1971
British Columbian Junior Athlete, 1972
Canadian Junior Athlete, 1972
Order of Canada Award, 1972: Presented by Roland Michener,
Governor General of Canada

4
What makes Leslie Swim? A question and answer in-depth interview with Leslie Cliff

In the previous chapter I talked about Leslie and how I believe she thinks and feels in relation to her ability, training, mental approach to swimming, etc. But I thought that it would be extremely valuable, both to coaches and competitors, if Leslie gave her own views of her swimming career. So I put the following questions to her—related both to swimming and competing generally and to individual medley specifically—and found her responses most interesting.

Q. *Swimming has played a very important part in your life. At what age and for what reasons did you first take up swimming ?*
A. I was three years old when my parents first enrolled me for lessons at our summer place at Crescent Beach. I took lessons every summer until I was eleven. When I started racing at five I trained just in the summer with a good coach, Bob Gair, and I thought I trained pretty hard. When I was eleven the coach there told me I should join the Canadian Dolphin Swim Club and swim all year round, and that's what I did.

Q. *What events did you compete in at first ?*
A. When I swam with my summer club I swam in all events because we were a team that went to championships and wanted to win. So the more races I swam the better. My specialities were freestyle and butterfly—I did better in those events.

Q. *What is your naturally strongest stroke ?*
A. I would have to say that butterfly is my naturally strongest

stroke, just because when I swam summer club that is the stroke I did best in—and that was when I didn't train.

Q. *Do you have a particularly weak stroke ? If you feel that you have, what have you done to try and improve it ?*
A. I have two weak strokes. Both my backstroke and breast-stroke are weak. I've learned how to swim the strokes and done a lot of skills on them and that is why I have overcome not being naturally talented in them.

Q. *When did you start to swim individual medley events seriously ?*
A. When I joined the Canadian Dolphin Swim Club I con-centrated on long-distance freestyle because that's where my best opportunities for making the National Championships team were—as is so often the case with a young swimmer. I enjoyed swimming a lot of events, so I started to swim 200 metres backstroke. I always swam 100 metres 'fly and I didn't really swim the breaststroke at all, but I did swim 100 metres and 200 metres freestyle and the individual medleys. Because I started to do better in the individual medleys I started to concentrate on them more—I realized I had an ability to do better there than in any other event. That's why I started specializing in it. I won the 200 individual medley at the Canadian Championships in 1970, so I started to take it seriously for the Pan-American trials in 1971, when I broke the Canadian record in the 200 I.M. And then about a week later I went to the United States Short Course Nationals, which were also the Pan-American trials. I placed third in the 200 yards and sixth in the 400 yards individual medleys. And that is when I started to think about it really seriously.

Q. *An individual medley swimmer must obviously be versatile and able to swim all four strokes well. Do you think it is necessary to specialize and train for individual medley in its own right ?*
A. I don't think it is necessary to specialize and train for individual medley at an early age. I don't think it matters

what strokes you work on when you are young, because whatever you do will help you when you are older, as individual medley combines all four strokes. But to be a good I.M.-er you do have to specialize in the event later on—but you still have to develop all four strokes individually both in workouts and in competition. No stroke must be neglected if you want to be a good individual medley competitor.

Q. *Individual medley is unique in that you must turn and change from one stroke to another. What problems does this present to you in a race and how do you overcome them in training and in competition?*
A. It presents a problem in that often you cannot concentrate when you first change strokes. Changing strokes is very difficult. For the first twenty yards or so it is hard to get your mind on what your are doing and not think about what you've just done or where you should be when you finish this stroke. It's really difficult, and the only way to overcome it is to practise changing from stroke to stroke and concentrate really hard on the first half-length of the new stroke. Following a turn, the second half of the new stroke is usually faster than the first half, because by that time you have built up a rhythm.

Q. *Why do you think you are a successful individual medley swimmer?*
A. If I am a successful I.M. swimmer it's because I practise all the strokes and all the skills involved—kicking, pulling, single arm on all four strokes—and I work for my best times in everything I do. I also practise changing from stroke to stroke, which obviously helps in I.M.

Q. *How has your training programme prepared you?*
A. My training programme has prepared me to do anything that comes up, because I swim with a lot of people in the pool and I have to be very flexible and work on any stroke that the group is given. It's prepared me to be very competitive because I am always fighting to be in a good place in the circle.

I like to lead out the circle whenever I can. It has obviously given me a lot of conditioning because we do a lot of work. It has taught me discipline in performing the programme as it was set out, and not to cheat on it. If I do the programme as it is set out I have confidence that I will swim well at the end, it's always worked out that way.

Q. *Do you enjoy workouts, or are they merely a means to an end?*
A. I enjoy workouts a lot, it's probably my main reason for continuing to swim. I enjoy them just as much as meets. There are many challenges in a workout, you can set up a lot of goals. You can try to do your best time in a 50-pull breaststroke, or anything. I know all my best times for all the skills—I really enjoy working out.

Q. *Do you enjoy working out as part of a group? Are there times of the year when you would like the group to be smaller? Do you accept it generally?*
A. I enjoy working out with a group very much—I wouldn't like to work out on my own or with only a small number of people, because there isn't the competition in the workout—you tend to think about only yourself and the clock and get pretty bored. When there are a lot of people there and everybody 'gets up' mentally ready to swim hard, everybody does swim hard and you don't notice just how hard you are really working, you are just trying to keep up with everyone else. But there are times during the year when I would maybe like to do a quality swim and I don't always get a chance when there isn't much room to do it. And at those times working as part of a large group can be a slight disadvantage. But the advantages really outweigh the disadvantages, because the group system keeps you really disciplined and very flexible, which is important. Because when we do go to swim meets, even to top-class competitions and to Nationals, conditions can be very difficult with hundreds of swimmers trying to warm up at the same time. This doesn't bother me because I am used to having to swim that way anyway.

Q. *Are you prepared to be competitive in every type of workout ?*
A. Yes, I try to work everything we do well. I usually don't slacken off in anything, whether it's pull breaststroke, backstroke kicking or anything, because I know that everything we do is important. I have trouble sometimes sprinting as well as I should, because I am not a natural sprinter. But I work just as hard at sprint workouts as I do on the distance repeats, which I am actually best at.

Q. *In your training programme you have to work with boys as well as with girls. How does working with them affect your swimming ?*
A. I like working with boys, because when there are just girls there I tend to just race against the swimmers too often and not race against the clock enough. And so when the boys are there I can race against them and my times will drop, because I'm racing against faster swimmers. When I get carried away with just trying to beat somebody I forget about my times. I really enjoy working out with the boys.

One of the disadvantages is that you can't lead out a circle, you can't control the circle because you are always trying to catch somebody and even if you swim great you're still not going to be able to lead the circle because the boys are always faster. That is the main disadvantage. And also, when you are swimming along against a boy and you feel tired and ready to give up, you are liable to think 'oh well, it's a boy anyway and I'm not expected to be with him.' If it were a girl you would not give up so easily.

Q. *How do you taper for a major event ?*
A. I start my taper about six weeks before a major event. And what I do is to rest more—I stop thinking about endurance and that type of training. I start thinking mentally about the race even six weeks before. I start maybe even having one whole workout just to get ready to do a quality broken 200 breaststroke or backstroke and doing a lot of long distance easy swimming working for good stroke technique. And I

maybe miss out a couple of morning workouts and get in a few massages. This is a gradual thing, but I could revert back to a couple of hard workouts after I've been tapering for $1\frac{1}{2}$ weeks or so. As the meet gets closer and closer I do less workouts and more sprinting with more rest. I lose a little weight during the taper and maybe a week before the major event, boost my sugar intake.

Q. *How do you feel before a race? What do you do in the hour or so before an event?*
A. So far I've felt different before every big race I've ever been in. I always feel a little nervous, sometimes more than at other times. Every big race that I've swum well in I've felt confident before I have swum and really gone in nervous, but not scared.

I usually get out of warm-up 45–30 minutes before a race, change suits, make sure I'm warm and I go and sit down somewhere and concentrate on the race. I may listen to conversations going on around me, and just try and stay relaxed and try and concentrate and have a good idea of what I'm going to do.

Q. *Do you have any strategy as far as a race plan is concerned in the individual medley?*
A. In the 400 metres I would like to get out and lead the whole way and win, but it's much easier to come from behind. It really depends on where your strengths and weaknesses are, where the other people's strengths and weaknesses lie, and how they compare.

Q. *You have a race plan before a race. If that plan is changed because the race itself is not going the way you expected it would, what do you do? Do you change your plan, or do you stay with it?*
A. So far I have been able to stay with the plan. I don't think I would have any difficulty in changing my idea of how to swim the race, because I've tried many different ideas in some of the less-important races and so built up the idea of what to expect swimming the race with different pace tactics.

Q. *What part does belonging to a good club play in your swimming ?*
A. Belonging to a good club, the Canadian Dolphins, plays a big part in my swimming because I have to swim so many things, perform so many skills and swim all the strokes. If I were swimming in a smaller club I think I would relax too much. But in the Dolphins we have world-class swimmers in all strokes and I can get beaten very easily if I don't 'put out' all the time—and not only by the boys, but by the girls as well.

Swimming for a good club really creates the feeling of team spirit in relays and things like that. Really the best thing I can have is a good club because it helps me in many ways. Competition in workouts, this is very important. And when I see somebody from my club swim well, it gives me confidence in our coach and in the programme and it makes me feel that what I'm doing is right too, even though I may not be swimming well at that particular time.

Because I belong to such a good club I feel more 'at home' at international meets because there are people I know working out around me. We had fourteen members of our club on the Munich Olympics team and this helped a lot by making me feel at ease.

Q. *Being a top-class swimmer has obviously made demands on you in terms of time etc. What problems have you had to contend with ?*
A. It could be easy to fall behind at school unless you are careful. Sometimes I was unable to work on my assignments as much as I should have done. I've missed a fair bit of time with my family—on holidays and just time with them. And a lot of social activities, such as parties or just being able to go to a movie with a couple of friends, you miss out on those things.

Q. *How have you overcome them ?*
A. I haven't really overcome the school problem. But the way to ease the problem is not to waste time at school at all

and to work really hard when you are there. There is no way to overcome the problem of the time you can't spend with your family and friends, because the time is just not there. But the time that you do spend with them is probably more enjoyable—you appreciate more the time you are able to spend together.

Q. *You are still training and competing at the age of eighteen when many girls quit in their mid-teens. What motivates you to continue—how has your interest been maintained?*
A. I guess what mainly keeps me in swimming is that I want to be one of the best swimmers in the world, so that keeps me going. But I also like training and I enjoy the workouts just as much as the big meets. I enjoy it, so why not do it, and why not keep doing it?

Also, the Canadian Government offers a lot of travelling trips, and I really enjoy the opportunity to meet other swimmers from different parts of the world. The reason I keep interested is that I'm sure that as yet I haven't done as well as I can do—I'm getting stronger and stronger each year, and there are so many things to develop in individual medley, there are so many skills and I still haven't mastered them all, so I still have a lot to work on and to achieve. There are also a lot of things to look forward to. That's what keeps me in it, I don't want to quit until I have achieved what I feel is my maximum potential.

Q. *What part do you think the following have played in your success?*
(i) *Natural talent?*
A. I don't like to admit it, but I don't think I have much natural talent at all. Maybe 30 per cent of what I have done is due to natural talent.

Q. (ii) *Your temperament: what personal qualities does a successful competitor need.*
A. I think that to be successful you have to be very competitive—always wanting to win—I've noticed that in most

swimmers. They even hate losing card games and things like that. Also, you need to be self-confident—not over confident, but confident, plus determined and flexible and not willing to give up just because things are not going your way.

Q. (iii) *Your parents?*
A. Almost no part, therefore a big part. They don't push, they just enquire how I'm doing, they encourage me in my decisions, but they never try to make any decisions for me.

Q. (iv) *School?*
A. As I said, I try to work hard while I'm at school. I've missed a lot of school, but usually my teachers have helped me to catch up, or have let me get away with a little bit, and so school hasn't really been a problem.

Q. (v) *Your coach?*
A. My coach has taught me how to swim—he has taught me the strokes, taught me a lot about tactics and races and things like that. Maybe he hasn't taught me competitiveness, that's something you are born with, but he has motivated me to swim well at the proper times. Probably 70 per cent of my success is due to him. As far as my relationship with my coach, it's hard to draw the line where your swimming life ends and your personal life begins. But our relationship is good in that it stays around swimming and the aspects of it.

Q. *Your first summer of International swimming was in 1970. Your first major event was the Commonwealth Games in Edinburgh. Would you like to give some ideas of how that summer affected you and what part it has played in your swimming?*
A. That summer has played a major part in my swimming. At the Commonwealth Games I felt that I was a very good swimmer, really confident, that I was one of the better swimmers in the world. But I was also a very nervous swimmer—the most nervous I have ever been. The night before

the final of the 200 metres backstroke, in which I came last, and the heats of the 400 metres individual medley, which I didn't make finals in, I don't think I slept. And regardless of how poor my times were, coming out of the meet I still thought I was a pretty good swimmer. But fortunately that summer Deryk took me to the U.S. Nationals in Los Angeles and I came almost last in everything I swam, which brought me back to reality. But it also brought me to the realization that I could be a great swimmer and I wanted to be a great swimmer very much. And that summer has really determined my swimming career so far.

Q. *Since then you haven't looked back. You won three gold and two silver medals in the 1971 Pan-American Games and a silver medal in Munich. What do you feel is your most satisfying achievement so far?*
A. I guess my medal in Munich was the best as a swimmer. But the most satisfying for me so far was winning the 200 metres individual medley in Cali, Colombia. It was a race that I didn't think I could win, but I did win it and it is the most satisfying race I've swum so far.

Q. *How do you feel after winning a major event? When you go back into training again, at the beginning of a new season, how does having won affect you?*
A. I've only won at the Pan-American Games and at the Nationals. But each time I felt really satisfied inside. I wasn't outwardly jumping around or anything like that, I just felt a really warm, rewarding feeling. Getting back to training after a big event like that usually affects my training in that . . . well, after the Pan-American Games I got over-confident and you forget how hard you worked to get where you did. And so it wasn't a good thing. After the American Nationals I think maybe I was a little over-confident again, but hopefully I have worked with a better understanding of the dangers of over-confidence. Confidence is one of the biggest things that all great swimmers have, maybe they are sometimes over-

Here Leslie Cliff is seen talking to interviewers after winning a race. Just one of the pressures of being a top competitor.

Deryk Snelling believes that a tough mental attitude as well as the physical ability to cope with situations helps his swimmers. Donna-Marie Gurr, who swam for more than six months with her leg in a plaster cast, went on to win a silver medal in the 200 metres backstroke at the Commonwealth Games.

Here Leslie is seen with some of her friends during an Australian tour, with the Sydney Harbour Bridge in the background. Left to right: Leslie, Karen James (Canada), Graham Windeatt (Australia), Shane Gould (Australia), Mike Wenden (Australia), Donna-Marie Gurr, Rose-Marie Pepe and Sue Smith (Canada).

The author (left) with Ralph Hutton, now one of his assistant coaches and former Olympic silver medallist.

confident, but it is so important to believe in yourself when you're in a race.

Q. *At the Olympic Games you had four events that you swam in —three of them ended up being major events, for you made the 200 metres backstroke final, the 200 metres individual medley and 400 metres I.M. finals. How did you manage to put this together to be able to taper for those events—how were they able to become so compatible ?*
A. They were so compatible because I had to sprint back-stroke in the individual medleys anyway, so maybe I put a little more emphasis on my backstroke sprinting than on any other stroke. But it really doesn't matter when you are getting down to sprinting what stroke you sprint, it's mainly the idea of really getting moving and just sprinting. Rest will obviously help you in any event and so they were really very compatible events.

Q. *How has swimming contributed to your all-round development as a person ?*
A. Swimming has made me healthy and physically strong. But it has also taught me a sense of achievement, self-confidence and a feeling that what I set my mind to do I can do and will do. The biggest reward for myself is self-satisfaction. But I have also been honoured at quite a few banquets and received the Order of Canada Medal and Canadian Junior Athlete of the Year award. But most important to me is the satisfaction that I have of just doing something and accomplishing something.

The travelling is really educational and interesting. I've been lucky enough to go to Brazil, Colombia, Australia, New Zealand and Europe and hope to go to some of these places again. By actually visiting different countries you learn so much more than sitting in a classroom and reading or hearing about them. But the best part has been meeting people and making friends throughout the world. It's a really nice feeling to know you have those friends.

Q. *What are your goals for the future?*
A. I set a lot of goals for myself, I get bored easily. I mainly set time goals—I want to break one minute for the 100 metres freestyle, break five minutes for the 400 metres individual medley, hold a world record. I like to set TIME goals, because when you set WINNING goals you are often deceiving yourself when the big race comes and goes. For instance, I won in Cali with a very slow time, and yet came second in Munich under the world record. And I have to look at the time to find out which race I have performed better in. And so I try not to set goals of winning, but just time standards—but of course I like to win too.

Q. *What advice would you give a young swimmer who wants to become an individual medley swimmer at International level?*
A. I guess the best advice is to be flexible and to compete in any and all events. Don't specialize in anything too early. It's a lot of work. On the technique side it's four times more work than that of a one-stroke swimmer. You cannot afford to neglect any skill on any stroke and you have to work on all of them equally. But mainly, in this day, to be a great individual medley swimmer you have to be prepared to swim longer than any other stroke swimmer, because there is so much more to develop, it just takes a lot longer and so you won't reach your full potential until you have been swimming the event for many years.

5

Our training programme so far: my own philosophies

The general philosophy of my programme revolves around a few important ideas, which are:

1. Motivation.
2. Trying to establish good attitudes towards group training and competition.
3. Fostering the idea of self-motivation. And that although each swimmer will receive support and experienced coaching, the swimmer himself will have to put in the work and have total commitment to the sport.

We have never been able to train in the way I would have really liked. Facilities have always been a problem—with a lack of space and difficulty in obtaining ideal pool time. We work as a group. Within the group we give everyone as much individual attention as possible, but the group concept is always dominant. Our main programme is carried out at Crystal Pool, Vancouver, a pool recreationally owned by the City. It measures 32 yards by 10 yards with a depth of 3 feet to 6 feet.

We work out five evenings a week, two from 5–8 p.m. and three from 5–7 p.m., and I consider these to be our main training sessions. In addition to this time, we work early mornings and at weekends whenever and wherever possible. In the summer we are able to step up our training by swimming outdoors. But the evening workouts are the sessions where most of our work is done.

During these training periods, we work a three-circle pattern, as this gives us maximum use of the pool with the numbers of swimmers involved. *At present I have three*

37

groups, which in a two-hour schedule gives each group forty minutes pooltime. I divide them up as follows:

'O' group have recorded times which qualify for U.S. Nationals.

'N' group have recorded times which qualify for Canadian Nationals.

'A' group have recorded times which qualify for local 'A' meets.

In addition to Crystal Pool we now have the use of a 25 metre pool where we have started to build up an age-group feeder club. I am really pleased with this idea, as it will provide us with 'new blood' for our senior programme in the future.

Coaches

I am lucky to have two good full-time coaches attached to the club. Don Dunfee is a great coach. Ralph Hutton, Canada's all-time great male swimmer is a real asset, as he is able to base his coaching on his own experience as an International competitor. He made finals in the 1964, 1968 and 1972 Olympic Games, winning a silver medal for Canada in Mexico. We also have several good part-time assistant coaches.

Facilities influence my programme

Our training is built around the idea of being a good club team and this has affected the way we have trained. For example, it takes more time and space to train swimmers for 800 metres and 1500 metres freestyle than it does to train for the sprints. As you score the same number of points for first place in a meet in the 100 metres as you do in the 1500 metres, we tend to concentrate on the shorter distances. Like all teams, we obviously aim to score as many points as possible when we go to a meet. So we have had to adapt our training pattern to the facilities available to us.

How does a 400 metre individual medley swimmer fit into this set-up?

The I.M. swimmer fits into this programme very easily, by

swimming the 100 or 200 workout programmes for all four strokes. This is basically the way that Dick Roth, George Haines' 1964 Olympic Champion, did it at Santa Clara and it is the way that we approach it with Leslie Cliff.

In our programme we work around the 200 metres distance, as I find that this is the most effective compromise to cover all events. From this, the 100 metres sprinters start their taper period earlier than the 200 metres competitors and suffer in no respect from working the 200 metres training programme.

Individual medley swimming is encouraged
At any workout all swimmers do the same stroke or practice at the same time. With limited space and time, this is the most satisfactory way of setting up a workable situation. And this brings me to a very important point. Because of the limitation on time, we must work hard at all times if we are to be in good shape. I HAVE FOUND THAT THE ONLY WAY I CAN BE SURE OF THIS IS TO ENCOURAGE EVERY MEMBER OF OUR TEAM TO BE AN INDIVIDUAL MEDLEY SWIMMER. At one time, when I didn't work this idea, swimmers would tend to work hard only on the stroke or strokes they swam in competition. A breaststroker wouldn't be too interested in the drills for freestyle and so on. For this reason, as much as 75 per cent of their training time could be considered as a virtual waste of time.

Using this concept of all swimmers training on all strokes has also helped me to spot a swimmer with a developing stroke more easily. For instance, a girl who has swum freestyle as a main event for several seasons, may turn out to excel in butterfly, and so on. For instance, Gudrun Wegner of East Germany, aged eighteen years—the first girl to swim 400 metres individual medley in under 5 minutes (World Aquatic Championships, Belgrade, 1973: 4: 57.51) was in fact a freestyler in 1972, swimming 200 metres freestyle in 2: 09.50, 400 f/s in 4: 23.10 and 800 f/s in 8: 58.90.

By working on the individual medley idea the risk of boring workouts is eliminated. However much time is put into planning varied workouts, it can be difficult to avoid tedium if all the time is given to one or even two strokes. I am not an exponent of specificity training except occasionally when it is necessary to specialize to make world standards for an all-important international event.

Workout philosophy

It is not compulsory to attend all our workouts in my training sessions, but everyone does. We don't worry too much about yardage swum. Good stroke form is stressed at all times. All our work is quality work and all done against the pace clock, whether it is kicking, pulling or full stroke.

Something we never have time for is warming up and warming down—we always start with a set, which is usually kicking. I feel the kicking is very important for my sprinters and individual medley swimmers, as it builds up stamina. It has been proven that the energy cost in a leg kick is two to four times higher than that of an arm stroke. In fact it may well be one of the best indicators to the fitness of a swimmer. It is also important for those who appear to be 'arms only' swimmers to do good leg practices, if only as a conditioner to guarantee a 100 per cent all-round conditioned body. 'If you can't kick them, run them,' said the late Bob Kiphuth, when asked how to train swimmers with limited pool time. The equally great and late Matt Mann was quick to add 'But don't run them if you can kick them!' In other words, use the pool time if you can get it.

Another point that I stress is that each swimmer works at his own level: that he tries to improve HIS OWN performance. Obviously swimming with competitors who are faster helps to pull times down. But to compare oneself with better performers too much can be very discouraging.

New ideas are important

I am constantly looking for new ideas and a better system. And because of this I am prepared to change our programme at any time. If a new idea comes along I try it and if it is successful I use it until something better comes along.

As far as fresh ideas are concerned a coach should always remember that methods he has used to train his top squad of swimmers are NEW IDEAS to the younger swimmers. But the one group that constantly needs new methods and ideas to stimulate them is the top group. At this stage something besides hard work and training is needed. Motivation plays a large part in determining just how far these top swimmers will go. This is something I shall discuss in more detail later.

Team unity

At all times the importance of the club is stressed. The only exception is in the case of the trials situation, where the object is to enable as many swimmers as possible to gain places on a National team. In this case individual swimmers have priority. And as I shall enlarge upon later, there is always room in our set-up for the star swimmer to come through.

We have a wide range of talent to cater for in our club, as is the case with most large swim clubs. One of the difficulties we experience with our young swimmers is created by the success of our top swimmers. For example, we placed fourteen of our swimmers on the 1972 Olympic team. With this kind of success more swimmers begin to realize their own potential. But as there are only a certain number of places available on National teams we have tried to fill a need for our hard-working swimmers who don't make these teams, as everyone in the club works hard. In fact quite often a harder working swimmer than another might not make the team. To keep these swimmers active and constantly interested we have created our own incentives, built around team travel.

So in our club set-up, all three groups have the opportunity to travel. For instance, in 1973 our top swimmers' goals were the First World Aquatic Championships in Belgrade, and the World Student Games in Moscow. The second group had a trip to Europe, including the English Championships. This was a three-week trip, and any members of the top group who didn't make Belgrade or Moscow had the opportunity to go along. The third group travelled down to California for ten days during the summer to compete.

To me, travelling out of province and abroad is necessary if you are to build a squad of great swimmers. Team travel is not only an incentive, but a necessity for the swimmer to reach for faster times and higher goals. And closely tied in with the idea of team travel is the philosophy of team spirit. The general philosophy of our club, and I believe one of our major assets, is our great feeling of team unity. We carry through this philosophy to the extent of always travelling and staying together as a team whenever possible, both at meets in Canada and on foreign tours. The swimmers have a common bond of club loyalty which I have always fostered. And while obviously striving for personal achievement, becoming rivals the second they step onto the starting blocks, they have the added incentive and responsibility of knowing they are contributing to a team effort.

Dolphin success: star swimmers will come through
It is important to understand that within this team concept, the individual swimmer does not suffer. The star competitor will always come through. We have had world class swimmers since the club was established in 1956 right through to the present time. Howard Firby was Head Coach from 1956 to 1967, when the first world class competitors started to emerge. The first were the Stewart sisters. Helen won a gold medal at the Pan-American Games in Mexico City and later in 1956 clocked 57.6 for 100 yards freestyle, a world record but one that was never ratified. Mary, who was seven years younger and much inspired by her sister, was world record holder in 100 yards and 100 metres butterfly.

Elaine Tanner was the most successful female swimmer at the 1966 Commonwealth Games, where aged fifteen she won four gold and three silver medals and broke two world records. She won gold medals in the 100 and 200 metres backstroke at the Pan-American Games in 1967, clocking world record times. In the 1968 Olympics she won two silver medals—100 and 200 metres backstroke. Elaine won 17 Canadian titles between 1965 and 1968. Jane Hughes, another member of the club, broke the world record for 880 yards freestyle.

More recently, Dolphins have won gold, silver and bronze medals at the Commonwealth, Pan-American and Olympic Games. Bruce Robertson became our first World Champion, winning the gold medal for the 100 metres butterfly at the World Aquatic Championships (55.6). Club members also include Wendy Cook (100 metres backstroke World Record—1:04.78), and sensational 16-year-old Steven Pickell (100 metres backstroke—57.6).

Club swimmers have won over 50 Canadian Championships and have set more than 300 Canadian records during the past six years, as well as winning U.S. individual national titles.

6

A dozen reasons why trips make a swim club go!

Our travels have taken us to many places. These include London, Amsterdam, Sydney, Dusseldorf, San Francisco, Wuppertal, Geneva, Cardiff, Dallas, Cincinnati, Edinburgh, Fiji, Hawaii, Brazil, Mexico, Colombia and many other places. And the trips have varied in length from a few days to being 'on the road' for over five weeks.

From these trips I have noted several important facts have emerged:

1. As soon as a trip is proposed, it immediately creates a new interest and incentive for swimmers to make the team.

2. Many swimmers for whom it is the first trip abroad, are exposed to a new and higher level of competition. They also learn much from their more experienced team mates.

3. It gives our more experienced competitors tougher competition—the level they need and will come up against in International competition.

4. With the longer tours, of three weeks or more, we learn to hold our performances with little time to train.

5. With increased experience on this type of trip, swimmers soon learn to relax and unwind for major competition.

6. During these trips swimmers come up against a wide variety of situations and conditions. They learn to become adaptable and perform well no matter what. One example of the kind of conditions with which a swimmer might have to cope was experienced in Cali, Colombia, at the Pan-American Games. We arrived to find that the swimmers were expected to sleep fourteen to a small room!

7. It is to the coach's advantage to be able to spend such a long period in constant close contact with his swimmers. It

makes for a better understanding between coach and swimmer.

8. Such trips are a great builder of team spirit.

9. On long trips there is a certain amount of stroke deterioration with many races and little opportunity to train.

10. Most swimmers are unable to produce a peak performance more than once a day. Other swims may be good but not outstanding. A swimmer often likes to decide beforehand where he is going to concentrate his efforts.

11. A swimmer who is in good shape generally races well on all strokes, even though he may have done little training on specific strokes.

12. Swimmers are prepared to train really hard provided there is a definite goal. I find that the idea of going to another country in six months' time or so acts as tremendous motivation. The swimmers are willing to get up early, train hard after school, give up parties and many of the social activities that would not be compatible with the programme, go to bed early and really give 100 per cent.

7
Separation of groups

There are three groups of individual medley swimmers within the programme:

1. Swimmers who are competing in individual medley events at National and International level.

2. Youngsters who are just beginning to explore the I.M. They can be exposed to all your ideas, because to them they are new ideas. Your assistant coach can take responsibility for this second group of swimmers. In this way he is able to take a personal interest in them by training and motivating them right through a complete programme. This squad might only be a year or so behind your top squad. This second group is usually a very 'tight' group. They train together and also travel together. This is probably an age-group squad primarily, working as a 'farm' group for your senior team. They will eventually replace the senior swimmers as they retire.

3. The third group of swimmers do not have heavy workout schedules. This group is just beginning to combine the four strokes to make the individual medley possible.

Within this group pattern, it is important that a swimmer is not moved into a higher group too soon. The coach should always recognize that there will be 'plateau' periods, where general consolidation is taking place without obvious progress. If a young swimmer is moved into a senior group too soon he will find that his strength and endurance will not hold up to the type of work being tackled. And this leads to demoralization: for after being one of the top performers in his own peer group the swimmer finds he is the tail swimmer in a circle. To avoid problems of this nature we have a clear dividing line between the groups and considerable thought is given before a swimmer is promoted.

8

The philosophy and psychology of mixed and unmixed workouts: what we do and what we don't do

In our workouts the girls and boys generally swim together, but on occasions they train separately. The girls prefer to train as a mixed group, but I find that the boys need to work out by themselves sometimes, as they then seem to have a more aggressive approach. For the girls, the challenges are greater during a mixed training session, but the boys are capable of destroying a workout if the girls press them too closely.

To make the most of the time available, instead of holding two separate workouts, a 'split' workout can be organized. This can be arranged by having the girls working from one end of the pool and the boys from the other. In this way the swimmers start off together and work the usual circle pattern. Two coaches are necessary if this is to work successfully, to organize and motivate.

Movement of the coach is important when working in a large pool. He should be in such a position that he can see every part of the pool and every swimmer in it. This is not always too easy, but it is absolutely necessary for effective control of the programme. It is important to move around and avoid staying on one spot for too long. If the swimmers know where to expect the coach they are likely to take advantage of that fact and maybe not work as well as they could. If a swimmer believes that he cannot be seen too well he is likely to 'cheat'. But if the coach is constantly changing his position in the pool the swimmers are more likely to be on their guard and more honest in their efforts.

What is cheating and when cheating becomes honest
I do not like a swimmer to cheat. It disturbs the other swimmers in the group if you do not spot those little moves that some swimmers always try and make, like cutting off the corner on a repeat when they believe you are not watching. We have a certain way of operating our workouts. This is that everyone in the group has to work equally. Each swimmer has to take his share of leading out a circle. I do not like anyone to cheat by leaving early on the clock. *But I do distinguish between two types of cheating:*

1. Cheating.
2. 'Honest' cheating.

For instance, we may be swimming an arms only drill without a band on the legs. If a swimmer kicks a little I don't mind as long as his effort is really good and he is kicking to try and win. But if he is cheating on the actual exercise, like cutting a corner, this is another thing altogether and something that I do not allow. I think there is quite a difference. Another example of 'honest' cheating is a swimmer who leaves early in a circle—for instance five seconds instead of a ten second interval. By leaving early he gets a fair amount of 'drag' and assistance from the swimmer ahead. But if this acts as motivation and gives the swimmer extra confidence, I accept this and look upon it as 'honest' cheating.

Time trials
I like to have a time trial event every Friday night—200 individual medley. It may come at the beginning, in the middle or at the end of the workout—whenever I feel the swimmers are ready. The reason for this is that I like to chart how well each swimmer is reacting to the type of work we are doing. Plotting the work load on a chart, for instance, can often tell you the expected performances a couple of weeks later. Now if a swimmer in the team cheats you can be reaching a completely wrong conclusion. In fact I may run through the test again for someone I feel is not putting the necessary 100 per

cent into the time trial. Often I do get the expected improvement, but I don't put the second time on the chart—the first attempt stands.

Occasionally, I like to call a stop to a practice and give a swimmer the chance to do a time trial swim if it looks as if there is the chance of a good time. It helps the whole team. First, the swimmer gets a chance to 'show off' a little, he gets the pool to himself (ideal conditions) and it gives the whole team a chance to stand and cheer a team-mate along. This should be used at sometime or other for just about everyone in the group from the fastest swimmer down to the slowest member of the team. But it should never be used to 'show someone up'. Always use it constructively.

Planning the circles
I find that with a very tough workout I have to plan the positions in the circle very carefully, particularly if I am going to run a $2\frac{1}{2}$ second interval between swimmers. I sometimes 'call' the positions from one down the line on best-ever times say over 100 metres in competition. This is usually effective if the distance is short regardless of how many repetitions we may swim. I would call this OBJECTIVE circle-seeding. It puts the lazy workout swimmer 'on the spot' and he has to work harder than usual just to stay in his place in the circle.

To create a real challenge I sometimes put the boys on a whole workout swimming arms only with a band on the legs, whilst the girls swim the full stroke. This really drives the boys mad and always makes for both good and competitive sessions.

Make the workouts interesting and fun!
Handicap swims can be worked. Always use ideas that don't take too much time and organization.

One of our toughest swims is width sprints over the 100. In our pool this is 10 widths swum against the clock. The girls can be tough at this if it is a series. The boys swim well if it is a short session but the girls have the ability to wear the boys down.

I use these different ideas to add interest to the programme. It is sometimes a little difficult for the swimmers to record this work in their log-books but if you ask for a few remarks at the end of each day's log, you will generally find that the good frame of mind this 'fun' approach puts the swimmers in is reflected in the comments.

Log-books

As a matter of interest, one thing we have found helpful in preparing log-books, is to use a different colour for good work and best times (red) and black for other times and comments. It helps both coach and swimmer to locate material more quickly.

9
Planning the programme: a season-long team training programme for Individual Medley swimmers

A: September–December
B: Xmas workshop and training camp
C: January–April
D: April–September

This programme has been responsible for producing a large number of successful individual medley swimmers at all levels, from age-group swimmers to international competitors. Such swimmers as Leslie Cliff and Bruce Robertson (gold medallist and World Champion in 100 metres butterfly at the World Aquatic Games, 1973) have put Canada 'on the swimming map.' And the depth of the programme is demonstrated by the team placings at the 1973 Canadian Championships. Canadian Dolphin girls placed first, second and third in the 400 individual medley finals. Leslie Cliff went 5:08.17; fifteen-year-old Jennifer McHugh swam 5:10.41 and fifteen-year-old Debbie Bengtson finished in 5:13.80. Six of the eight finalists in the men's 200 metres individual medley were Dolphins. And our girls filled the six I.M. places on the 1972 Olympic team.

I like to divide my swimming year up into two seasons:
1. *September–April: winter season*
   Our goal during this period is the U.S. Nationals.
2. *April–September: summer season*

Our goals are the Canadian Nationals and the major Games.

A. *September–December*
Diet
During this period we work on getting back into shape after our summer vacation. We aim to lose any excess weight, working on the idea that our best racing weight is the weight we swam at when recording our best time in competition during the last season. We have no special diets. But if we have been unable to achieve our ideal weight through exercise and training we watch the calorie intake in cases of over-weight. For this I recommend charting the daily food intake for one week to establish present calorie consumption, rather than using the regular type of chart which gives ideal calorie intake for specific heights and builds. From this chart we work out how to adjust (lower) the normal intake of calories to lose about two pounds a week. This is approximately equal to a reduction by 1200–1500 calories per day, or 8400–10,000 a week. It is definitely a mistake, especially for a swimmer or anyone engaged in heavy physical training, to avoid eating any of the three essential food groups completely (fats, carbo-hydrates, proteins). The philosophy should be reduction, not elimination.

Tests and measurements
Our only venture into the field of testing was made during this period in 1972. The Department of Kinesiology, Simon Fraser University (led by Dr. Eric Banister) helped us with somatotype rating and fat testing. For these tests, a cross-section of the club acted as 'guinea pigs'.

Tests and measurements are interesting, but have little value to us unless they are followed up practically. The fat test scale shows the per cent of fat on the body—and this is broken down into specific areas, which is important. This gives an exact indication of the areas of the body which are overweight. When this is known, action can then be taken to reduce the fat in that part of the body by exercise. Whereas reduction of food intake can reduce weight generally, it gives us no control over the body area from which we lose the weight. By taking care with diet and also doing exercises to reduce in certain regions, we do have some control over this. For instance, one subject of the test was found to be considerably overweight in the abdominal region. By doing exercises to reduce and strengthen this area, such as sit-ups, leg-raises, etc., he was able to get back into top physical shape without losing strength and bulk where he needed it.

Another important factor in testing is to have somebody other than the coach to do the testing in order not to use up valuable pool time. Testing can be both interesting and useful if a nearby university can provide the testing personnel. Your testing must be positive and convince the swimmer it is giving him some new 'edge'—an advantage because his training is more scientific than that of his opposition.

Land work

We start on our land work during this period, September–December. This consists of general exercises (calisthenics), work with pulleys, weights (a little), flexibility exercises, isometrics and exergenie. I have included the exercises that we use in chapter 12, as I feel that although we don't have a heavy land conditioning programme—due mainly to lack of time and space—it is a valuable and necessary part of any swimming programme.

This September–Xmas period is a great time for us. It is the most relaxed time of the whole year. It is the time of year when we have a lot of time to think about our strokes and our goals and objectives for the coming year. And we have time to concentrate on even making major changes to stroke technique, turning skills, etc.

We work this part of the season in the following way:
Most of our training takes place during the evening—we don't concentrate on double workouts at this time of the

season. The idea of this is that with only one workout a day all swimmers come in very fresh and really interested. They have considerable time to adjust to getting back into the water and there is no real stress or strain involved.

I like to swim our practices over short distances. I find that if we go swims of one length at a time we are able to really concentrate on stroke technique. There is no need for endurance work at this time of the year. We do this later in the season when we can go two workouts a day and really have an objective in the conditioning part of the season. We do lots of sprint work—times come down more easily during lighter training periods. We train for speed during these winter months. We then try to 'hold' these times during the intensive training period later on, when yardage becomes an important factor.

We concentrate on one aspect at a time. I usually try to work three sessions in a row on the same stroke. The first session is introductory, starting with the skills involved. The second practice is a follow-up of the first one. At this stage it is easy for the swimmers to understand what they were not able to achieve in the first practice, so this workout is usually a little better on the stroke technique. And by the time we reach the third consecutive practice each swimmer is really beginning to 'get the feel' of the stroke. I believe in concentrating on the one stroke at a time. This way there are no other distractions, the mind is very clear and able to see just the one picture. If, at the end of the three sessions, I feel that the swimmers have really been able to 'get hold' of the new idea on which we have been working, we might take a morning workout and go longer repeats on the full stroke—not swimming fast but trying to hold the rhythm and the technique.

Technique and stroke drills
Technique is very individual. And when training a large group of swimmers and giving stroke practice, I have found that the best results come from what I call 'skill practices'. These skill practices are sometimes just an extension of the well-

known practices for arms only or legs only. But I have found that by breaking the stroke down into as many parts as possible, we have been able to really concentrate on the technique refinements of that stroke, breaking down the stroke and then rebuilding it step by step with drills that will not allow old mistakes to creep back in.

Butterfly
three phases—
1. Kicking
2. Pulling
3. Full stroke

1. Kicking
(i) *Dolphin kick,* with the face in the water and the arms down by the sides. By having the head down the swimmer is able to get a good pike and the hips really high. And there is a good feeling of moving up and down.

(ii) *Dolphin kick,* arms extended out in front, but using no support from a board—just keep the thumbs locked together, the feet together—concentrate on the different aspects of the kick—keep the knees together, the ankles extended and the feet actually touching each other. To breathe while doing this particular practice we take a short breaststroke pull when we are ready to lift the head for breath.

(iii) *Lie on the back, hands down by the sides.* The idea of doing the dolphin kick in this position is that by having the face clear of the water the whole time the swimmer is able to breathe naturally. He is able to concentrate on actually seeing how the lower part of the leg really works. Bring the feet up strongly in the up-thrust, which means there is a lot of pressure against the instep of the foot—feel the idea of whipping.

(iv) *Lie on the side in the water.* This practice can be done either completely submerged for short distances, or can be swum over a longer distance lying on the side with the chin turned inward towards the shoulder, breathing in this position.

The body is at 90° to the surface. In this position the swimmer is able to feel the sensation of forward propulsion rather than up and down movement. This gives an idea of how to push the water directly backwards.

(v) *Using kickboards:* Our usual practice is to have one kickboard out in front, keeping the arms extended over it with the head up the whole time. We just kick normally. The emphasis here is on a very deep bend at the knees, so that there is an obvious working of the thighs as well as the ankles flipping the water. One of the problems is often caused by the knees spreading too far apart. To prevent this we use a band around the knees to hold them together. It is important that this practice is swum with the knees together. A practice that I have introduced recently to bring the swimmer into different body positions has, I feel, been very successful. We place TWO KICKBOARDS together, fastened with a band. This makes the swimmer arch the back a little more and with this arch the lower back is having to work in the sort of position experienced when performing the whole stroke. We also use a THREE-BOARD COMBINATION for the same reason, and this is particularly good for sprinters. Most of the swimmers have to practise with back exercises such as back-arches with a weight behind the head (face down). In this exercise the chest is lifted as high off the ground as possible. A butterfly swimmer must be strong in the lower back and I have found that these exercises help our butterfly swimmers, particularly the sprinters, who like to be able to arch and get high out of the water for their stroke.

2. Pulling

(i) *Single-arm butterfly*—the main pulling practice that we use with our butterfly swimmers. The idea of using this practice is that every swimmer on the team is able to swim quite long repeats, not only the main stroke butterfly swimmers. It also works well in a crowded situation, so we use it a lot, swimming in our tight circles.

(ii) *Start with both arms forward in the extended position,* hands together. Hold the stationary arm out in front at surface level. The working arm makes the pull down the normal line for the butterfly stroke. As the hand reaches down towards the thigh in the push-back, turn the head on the side to inhale. As the hand clears the water at the end of the release, concentrate on keeping the elbow straight. The arm rotates from the shoulder with a straight elbow, the hand lifted up as high as possible, just as though you are reaching for the ceiling. Keep that arm swinging in a perfectly high arc over from behind the back, past the side of the head and coming straight in line with the centre position for entry. Thus the arm has followed a half-circle in a vertical plane. Kick normally during this arm cycle, with two kicks to the one arm pull. This can be swum very fast and quite competitively and is particularly suitable for crowded workouts with many swimmers in the water at the same time. We also use this during individual medley repeats. It can be worked in several ways. For instance, the first length can be swum with the right arm, the second length with the left arm, and so on. Or it can be worked on three pulls with one arm, followed by three pulls with the other arm. Or any other combination can be used.

(iii) *Single-arm butterfly*, free arm down by side. (Done as above.)

(iv) (a) single-arm, one pull on the right side.

    (b) single-arm, one pull on the left side.

    (c) one full stroke.

    (d) arms finishing in a front-pause position.

(v) As (iv) but with arms pausing down by the sides.

ALL THE ABOVE DRILLS CAN BE DONE WITH OR WITHOUT PADDLES.

3. Full stroke

(i) *Dive butterfly:* for inexperienced or even moderately good butterfly swimmers to be able to swim any reasonable distance, I have found that some of the strain has to be taken out of the stroke. We do this by creating what I call 'dive butterfly'. The swimmer makes a deep dive as the hands enter the water, allowing the whole body to go below the surface of the water to about 2 ft. to 2 ft. 6 in. With the arms extended out in front, put five or six kicks into the underwater phase and make the surface stroke, take a breath, dive again and kick five or six times. We do this up and down the pool over a variety of distances. This diving stroke obviously requires good breathing practices, as the swimmer is underwater for two or three seconds at a time. But there is very little strain on the arms. *Once a swimmer can cover 200 metres using this particular type of stroking,* the next step is to continue with 'dive butterfly', but make the dive a little more shallow, in fact only just below the surface. Three to four kicks are allowed, but no more than four. And this is beginning to relate much more to the full stroke—and towards building the normal stroke of two kicks to one pull. But it is still much easier than performing the regular butterfly stroke. The emphasis in this skill is on forward motion, rather than the deep pitching and diving of the previous skill. Once I feel that the swimmer can hold this reasonably well, we start alternating this shallow, dive-stroke with the normal full stroke on the surface.

A typical combination for 200 metres is: the first 25 metres is full stroke, swum with the deep diving stroke (i); the second 25 metres is full stroke; the third 25 metres is practice (i) again; the fourth is full stroke, and so on for 200 metres.

The above skills are usually used only for swimmers who are not main butterfly swimmers or those who do not have natural butterflying ability. And the outlined drills are ideal for the typical breaststroker who cannot perform the butterfly too well. Such swimmers can, using the modifications I have talked about, fit into working with the individual medley swimmers who are swimming all four strokes, quite quickly.

When we are swimming the full stroke we keep most of our repeats down to one-length swims, sometimes with short rests, sometimes with long rests, changing the breathing pattern, but usually working on one breath for one stroke or one breath for two strokes. *In fact, we use three breathing patterns:*

(a) Breathe each stroke.
(b) Breathe every second stroke.
(c) Breathe in a rhythmical pattern—two single strokes, followed by two double strokes between each breath.

WHEN THIS STROKE IS MASTERED WE HAVE THE TECHNIQUE FOR THE FIRST QUARTER OF THE INDIVIDUAL MEDLEY. IF IT HAPPENS TO HAVE BEEN THE WEAK STROKE OF A SWIMMER'S I.M., THEN THIS IS CERTAINLY THE TIME OF THE YEAR TO CORRECT IT.

THE SECOND STROKE IN THE INDIVIDUAL MEDLEY IS BACKSTROKE —THE MOST LOGICAL AND THE ACTUAL FOLLOW-UP TO BUTTERFLY IN THE I.M.'S FOUR-STROKE SEQUENCE.

Backstroke
three phases—
1. Kicking
2. Pulling
3. Full stroke

1. Kicking
(i) *Arms down by the sides*, kick normally keeping the knees just below the surface and watch the 'white water' and the feet. I find that it helps our sprinters to have their arms by their sides as they assume a 'sitting position' and therefore have a slightly deeper leg-kick.
(ii) *This is a very flat position*, with the head well back and the arms extended over the head and the hands locked together. This is the position that is most streamlined, and more suitable for the 200 metres backstroker who would probably use it more often than the deeper 'sitting' position.
(iii) *In order to measure the efficiency of the kick* we use a third kicking practice for backstroke. The swimmer lies in the normal backstroke position, arms extended straight up above the head at right angles to the body. I find that if a backstroker can kick in this position without sinking below the surface he has a good feeling for buoyancy and body position and is certainly working his legs very efficiently. But we only use this

practice occasionally, mainly as a test of strength and efficiency.
(iv) *Kicking lying on the side,* chin turned into the shoulder.

During these kicking practices we:
(a) Hold head at different angles.
(b) Hold hips at different depths.
(c) Kick with knees at different degrees of bend.

2. Pulling

We use 'arms only' practices mainly for strengthening purposes. We do this with the feet fastened with a rubber band,
rather than a tube, as I find the tube brings the swimmer a
little too high in the water. We also use the hand paddles a
lot for our backstroke work and also 'single-arm' backstroke.
I believe that by isolating one aspect of a skill the swimmer is
able to concentrate and learn the whole skill more easily.
We use two positions when swimming the single-arm:
(i) Extend the stationary arm above the head and use it as a
guide for the entering hand to find the centre line. Having the
arm extended helps to keep the swimmer very flat in the
water. This helps to 'balance out' a swimmer who is rolling
too much. This position helps him to feel just how to lie flat
and to keep a good body position.
(ii) *In this drill the stationary arm is kept down by the side of the
body.* As the working arm is pulling, the opposite shoulder
should be raised above the water, giving the impression of
trying to clear the whole arm out of the water. This allows a
little movement of the body and in fact raising the free shoulder
just clear of the water during the pulling phase enables the
swimmer to get good depth of pull. This is a good drill for the
swimmer who is having trouble getting the shoulders out of
the water on the recovery arm. Again, the number of pulls
can be varied, from a few pulls on one arm followed by the
same number on the other, to a length or more on each side.
(iii) *Double-arm backstroke.* In this practice both arms are
recovered simultaneously above the surface. The arms
enter the water with the backs of the hands together, elbows

straight, then the hands are pressed down into the water. This is a very good shoulder mobility exercise. As the head is held high there is a very good feeling of an early 'catch' and the stroke is very symmetrical down the pull. This helps a swimmer who has had trouble with a bent arm on one side and a straight arm on the other. The most important part of this skill is from the middle to the end of the stroke. Try to push down, holding the water with the forearm and the hand. Push down towards the feet, but keep the stroke wide at the bottom. Use the normal backstroke kick.

3. Full stroke
On occasions we use practices like 'catch-up' stroke. For this one arm is held out in front, while the other arm makes a complete cycle. The stationary arm does not start its pull until the working arm has come back into line with the centre entry position. This practice helps a swimmer who is not feeling the correct position and is cutting the stroke short at the top.

THE THIRD QUARTER OF THE INDIVIDUAL MEDLEY, BREASTSTROKE, IS SO DIFFERENT FROM THE OTHER STROKES AND CAN EITHER BE A REST OR A 'DRAG', DEPENDING ON HOW WELL IT IS SWUM. EFFICIENCY IS IMPORTANT AND SWIMMERS TEND TO BE EITHER NATURAL OR IMPOSSIBLE BREASTSTROKERS. IF THE LATTER, THEN AGAIN THIS IS CERTAINLY THE TIME OF YEAR TO RE-LEARN IT SO THAT IT WILL BE A HELP RATHER THAN A HINDERANCE IN INDIVIDUAL MEDLEYS LATER IN THE SEASON.

Breaststroke
three phases—
1. Kicking
2. Pulling
3. Full stroke

1. Kicking
(i) *Kicking holding wall,* horizontal body position.

(ii) *Kicking holding wall,* vertical body position, body pressed flat against the wall.

(iii) *Kick with board held in vertical position.* This is a high-resistance exercise.

(iv) *Kick lying on the back,* arms by sides, heels drawing up to touch the hands.

(v) *Kick with rubber band around knees.* This is a good practice for developing a narrow-leg whip-kick.

(vi) *Kick in deep water*—'egg-beater'—vertical position.

(vii) *Kick in deep water*—two-leg 'egg-beater'—arms extended above the head, in a vertical position.

(viii) *Kicking using three different board-combinations,* one, two and three boards. The high boards help to keep the shoulders up above the water and encourage a strong back-arch. The body is able to work well from the hips down in this position.

(ix) *Kicking without a board, thumbs locked together,* arms extended. The emphasis here is on a very strong breaststroke leg-kick.

(x) *Kicking holding the arms down by the sides.* Feel the heels coming up to touch the fingers. We only use this practice on occasions, but I do find it has some value.

2. Pulling

(i) The object of this first practice is to get a very fast turnover with the arms. This is as much a strength and speed practice as a stroke drill. *Swim pulling the full breaststroke arm action, but as fast as possible.* Allow the legs to trail behind and in fact don't discourage the idea of a little dolphin kick which co-ordinates with the driving forward of the hands in recovery.

(ii) *Lie horizontal just under the surface of the water,* legs spread apart in 'V' shape. Allow the head, hips and heels to stay right up on the surface. This is a very good practice for keeping the head, shoulders and body flat on the surface. It also eliminates any additional thrust from the legs. With the wide leg position we get a lot of resistance and it becomes a much more difficult drill and a very honest indication of strength and efficiency. Start with the hands near the surface as the pull press-down starts. But catch the water very early, as early as in the first one or two inches, as the hands start to spread from the centre position in the pull-back.

(iii) *Pulling with straight arms, very wide*. Pull and breathe at the end of the pull.

(iv) Pulling, using a pull-buoy for flotation.

3. Full stroke (co-ordination)

We use the usual type of skill practices for the full stroke, where we take long glide strokes and gradually build up the speed of the turnover and eventually eliminate the glide completely, but never eliminating the extension in the stroke.

(i) *Alternating single-arm pull action,* fitting in with the normal kick.

(ii) *Alternating single leg-kicks,* fitting in with the normal stroke.

(iii) *Two kicks, one pull* and other multiples.

(iv) *Two pulls, one kick* and other multiples.

(v) *Normal stroke,* but following the extension do dolphin whip.

I also like to swim parts of our practices under water. This helps with under water stroking technique and breath-control. To develop strength and speed do quality swims in widths.

The dry land exercises for breaststroke are different in that squat jumps, bicycle riding, figure skating, ballet—even limbo dancing—will help the leg-kick unnatural to many swimmers. If a swimmer just doesn't 'have it' on the breast-stroke kick we try a butterfly/dolphin with the toes turned out. With good push-offs, a good under-water stroke and a good pull, an individual medley swimmer can get by with this 'substandard' breaststroke-kick, without wearing out before the freestyle finish.

THE COMPETITOR WHO FINISHES FIRST IN THE INDIVIDUAL MEDLEY IS USUALLY THE ONE WITH THE MOST EFFICIENT

FRONT CRAWL WHEN HE IS TIRED. WE WORK ON THIS STROKE IN THE AUTUMN (FALL) IN THE FOLLOWING WAY:

Front Crawl
three phases—
1. Kicking
2. Pulling
3. Full stroke

1. Kicking
We always practise front crawl kicking on boards, again with the same combination of one, two or three boards. We often vary the type of freestyle kick as far as depth is concerned. Sometimes the kick is shallow and fast, in fact breaking the surface of the water. But part of the time I insist on really strong, deep kicking—not allowing the feet to break the surface at any time. With both practices, the movement is the same, initiated from the hips, working through the knees with good extension and whipping action of the feet.

2. Pulling
We work on arms only with a rubber band around the ankles, over distances ranging from 25 metres to 3000 metres. We do use flotation when doing arms only-drills. We use the pull-buoys and inflated tubes, but only when a swimmer has great difficulty in doing the proper arm-action without.

We count the number of stroke pulls in a lap—I find that stroke counting is important on arms-only front crawl as the strokes have to be effective and this should be measured—this is our way of doing it. The paddles can also be added as an extra overload (increasing the work-load) but usually the band itself is adequate for this practice.

I feel that it is very important for individual medley swimmers to have a strong and efficient pulling action. For quite often at the end of a 400 metres race, following the breast-stroke, a lot of the strength and feeling has left the legs. And sometimes the swimmer has to be able to bring the race home with heavy emphasis on the arms. So a lot of pulling in practice is important.

The breathing pattern should be changed consistently, with as much work as possible on bilateral practices, breathing every third arm-pull.

Emphasize a high head position in arms-only exercises. The tendency is to make the pulling position more horizontal by burying the head, allowing the legs to float up high behind, changing the centre of gravity. This is not a good position, and certainly not a position from which we gain most benefit in these arms-only pulling exercises. Work on a high elbow position in recovery, making the turn-over faster than would normally be used in the full stroke.

3. Full Stroke
The pulling position is the same for the full stroke, but with a slightly more shallow pull, particularly in the front phase of the stroke and as the hand comes underneath the head.
(i) *Single-arm freestyle*, free arm extended out in front.
(ii) *Catch-up stroke:* both arms start in the forward extended position—one arm remaining in this position. The pulling arm makes a full cycle through pull and recovery back to the forward position. There is a slight pause before the opposite arm makes its cycle.
(iii) Riding with one arm resting on a board, free arm entering just ahead of the kick-board—arm pulling under the board. This is a practice for the completion of the push-through phase. This is an excellerating movement, finishing very strongly at the back end of the stroke. The whole exercise should be done at sprint pace.
(iv) *Extension-stroke:* this is a pause-stroke, where the cycle has a stop-phase with one arm in the forward extended position, the other in a backward extended position. The normal leg-kick continues through this arm-pause position.

How to develop your individual medley swimmers from this programme
As I mentioned earlier, when a swimmer has mastered the stroke skills and has a basic understanding of butterfly,

backstroke, breaststroke and freestyle, I believe he is ready to work seriously on the I.M. as an event. At this point swim meets start to play an important part in the development of the individual medley.

Swim meets provide excellent preparation
I use the swim meets as quality training for our swimmers, entering the 'I.M.-er' in every event, or almost every event, in the programme. This is initially extremely hard for the competitor and there are two things that I try to impress on him:
(i) Every event is important.
(ii) Although many events are swum, he should concentrate on good performances in certain events and just 'swim through' others. It is impossible at this stage to give exceptional performances in every race.

In a good meet, with a full programme, a swimmer who competes in heats and finals will swim more than 5,000 metres of 'quality training', plus the warm-ups and swim-downs. This can be extremely tough, both physically and mentally, over a two-day meet. But I have found that over a period of four or five meets on consecutive weekends, provided the swimmer can take Fridays and Mondays out of the water to rest, the individual medley prospect can make considerable progress on this programme.

The mental drain of this type of intensive programme can be enormous, especially at first. But the experience is invaluable. Certainly the swimmer must be given to understand why he is doing this and not resting after one or two events. Once he understands, the satisfaction can be great. It becomes a game of toughness and it actually adds up to less pressure, not more, and gives greater ability to handle pressure later when the swimmer is down to one or two events a day. I find that if a swimmer responds well under this type of stress and once he has had a period of rest he will be really 'sharp' and swim really well in the end-of-season meets. Another advantage can be seen for the swimmer who has maybe one or even

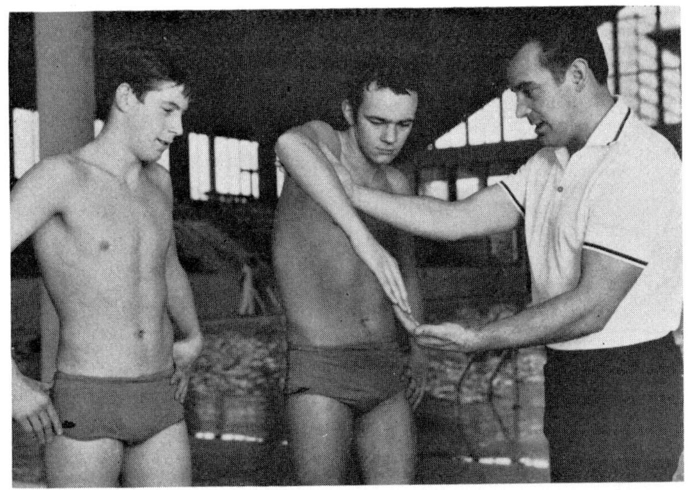

Snelling constantly stresses stroke form in his workouts. Here he is seen with two of his early individual medley champions, Ray Terrell (left) and Alan Kimber of Great Britain.

'To me travelling out of province and abroad is necessary if you are to build a squad of great swimmers', believes Snelling. 'Team travel is not only an incentive but a necessity for the swimmer to reach for faster times and higher goals.'

Left. *Elaine Tanner, member of the C.D.S.C. who broke the world records in the 100 and 200 metres backstroke. She held five world records in her swimming career and represented Canada many times.*

Left. *Helen and Mary Stuart. Helen clocked 57.6 for 100 yards freestyle in 1956, a world record, but one that was never ratified. Mary, who is seven years younger and much inspired by her sister, was world record holder in 100 yards and 100 metres butterfly.*

two strokes that are 'in a rut'. By swimming many different events and distances he does not have time for 'negative dwelling' on poor races.

This is also ideal I.M. training when individual medley events are not included in these early meets. By swimming all four strokes, especially when events are close together, it can be looked upon as broken I.M. swimming.

It is important for swimmer and coach to follow up each meet—that they discuss each performance—every split of every event—and that communication is constantly available between each race. If worked carefully and correctly this system is ideal for the building of individual medley competitors.

B: Xmas workshop and training camp
This is a training camp which I run during the school vacation. It is the main starter and pre-conditioner for the whole December–April competition period. I believe in it. This vacation time must be fully used and preferably doing something quite different from your usual workouts. In Eastern Canada and the U.S. many teams go to Florida for this break in training routine. We are $400 per person too far away from this, so I try to make it fun at home.
Venue: 25 metres pool, with a gymnasium and weight-training room.
Time: 10 days during the Xmas vacation. We work every day except Xmas Day, running from 8.00 a.m.–4.00 p.m. with only a short break for a packed lunch. We use this time for discussions/lectures and films.

Type of discussions and lectures
(a) Physiology.
(b) Diet.
(c) Psychological aspects of competition.
(d) Stroke technique.
(e) Pacing and race strategy.
(f) Values of goal-setting.

(g) Prospects for the coming season—travel, national teams, dates of meets, etc.

Topics of films
(a) Swimming technique.
(b) Track and field films and any films which are available to us that will motivate—such as Lombardi on football, film of the Olympic Games, etc.
(c) Films we have taken on our own trips. These are always interesting and popular as they recall the achievements and happy memories of both past and present club members.

A Typical Day

8.00–10.00	:	Swim
10.00–11.00	:	Weight training
11.00–12.00	:	Run or circuit
12.00–12.45	:	Ball game in gymnasium
12.45– 1.30	:	Lunch and lecture
1.30– 2.15	:	Calisthenics
2.15– 4.00	:	Swim

We have the opportunity to use the video-tape during the swimming sessions.

Weight training
As I mentioned earlier, we have little opportunity to train with weights during most of the year. But at Xmas we have full use of a weight-training room and we do some work each day with weights. Examples of the weight-training exercises we use during this workshop and throughout the season are given in the chapter 'Land Conditioning Exercises'.

Running
Running is good for endurance and stamina, but should be built up easily to avoid shin splints, ankle trouble, etc. The swimmer is particularly prone to joint injury on land, especially ankles, due to the desired suppleness and looseness of joints. We run anything from 200 yards up to five or six miles,

according to time and the ability of the group. We jog, run fartlek and sprint.

Calisthenics
Examples of the type of exercises we work on are given in Chapter 12.

If anything, I think the ball games must be the most popular aspect of the workshop. The games are always fun and rough. I think our girls' floor hockey team would really frighten the Montreal Canadiens if a match could ever be arranged!

After ten days of this kind of training, we are in good shape for the middle of the winter period. It also encourages team spirit and gives swimmers a real chance to get to know one another out of the pool situation—between forty and seventy of my swimmers attend the clinic.

When running this kind of course and working the type of programme I am outlining, it is a good idea to meet with parents and swimmers before the season begins. This gives them an idea about the dates of important meets and the type of programme as well as the time involved. At the same time you may want to send them off with your blessing, but feeling a little guilty if they don't do something active during their Christmas vacation in California or Hawaii—'By all means go, but don't get behind or you may sink when you hit the pool in January!'

Certainly the kids who stay home have fun and feel their Christmas holiday more accomplished when they have survived our workshop.

C: January–April
This is when our programme really starts to develop and hold the interest of the senior swimmers. They are easily motivated and this is important with the heavier and longer training periods coming up. Self-motivation is also evident. It seems that following the Xmas training camp and at the start of a new year, the goals that we have talked about for many months start to become more real. We now start the double training

sessions—morning and evening workouts—usually concentrating on the longer distance repeats in the morning and working towards speed, broken swims and effort performances in the evening.

Although we are doing two practices a day during this period, our objective is not yardage. I find that if I emphasise yardage, we are likely to neglect part of the strokes which are important in the individual medley, particularly the leg-kicks. Everyone knows that leg-kick practices are going to take up much more time and cover less yardage. But without good leg-kicks on all four strokes, the swimmers don't really have the ability to control the rhythm and timing of all four strokes. Conditioning is time in the water and how hard you work it, but not necessarily yardage.

During the early part of the January/February training period we do a lot of kicking practices. Kicking distances vary from 32 yard sprints up to 1,500 yards. The same multiple of repeats is worked on kicking as on full stroke. We don't always keep an even balance on kicking work. But one stroke that I make absolutely sure to include in all workouts is the breaststroke. I feel that the breaststroke is one of the main keys to a good individual medley performance. And without a good breaststroke leg-kick, the stroke rhythm and timing is not what is desired. Kicking worked as a squad can be very competitive. Individual swimmers are able to pace themselves much better if you use two clocks, one at each end of the pool. Each swimmer can concentrate on every split and know just where the pace is dropping off and can then adjust on the next repeat or set to achieve a good, steady pace.

We don't swim a lot of individual medleys in our workouts due to the lack of space. But whenever possible, if I have a small group in the water, I take full advantage of this and work on the I.M. as a complete event.

Broken swims for individual medley
When we are doing a specific individual medley workout I like to work broken swims. Swims can be broken at 25 and 50,

100 or 200 metres, using any type of stroke combination. So long as each swimmer knows his own practice time for each stroke and distance this training is constructive and valuable. It helps each swimmer to learn about pace. It is important, if full benefit is to be gained, that the coach is active in giving swimmers coaching advice between swims. We work these broken swims with legs only, arms only and full stroke.

One popular way of working these broken individual medley swims is:
100 metres butterfly—single arm
100 metres backstroke—single arm
100 metres breaststroke—arms only
100 metres freestyle—full stroke
If this is being worked with a small group of swimmers in the water and the times are controlled by giving a ten-second interval between 100's, this is fine. But we are often working in a large group situation. So to work this on a circle pattern we use a turnover interval.

Our intervals on the yards swims would be:
Butterfly—$1\frac{1}{2}$ minutes
Backstroke—$1\frac{1}{2}$ minutes
Breaststroke—1 min. 45 secs.
This way all swimmers can keep a clearer check of their times. Also, the coach is able to keep track of the whole group. I find it easy to follow 16–20 swimmers on this type of turnover interval. And to know each of their specific splits. By knowing the splits a coach is able to be more functional in the feed-back he is able to give each swimmer.

We usually work these broken 400's as a set. A set usually ranges from three to eight 400's swum in this pattern. The workout times that I set depend on how I feel a particular swimmer is going on a particular day, taking circumstances such as school, sickness, fatigue, etc. into account.

The type of work I have outlined for I.M. is usually used well into the season, when much mileage has been put in on all four strokes and each swimmer is able to turn in a balanced performance.

I always like to try and finish each workout in such a way that every swimmer has the chance to turn in a good performance. This is not necessarily a sprint. But before this final effort I allow a slightly longer rest and encourage the group to attack the swim aggressively. I like each swimmer to get out of the water feeling as though he has achieved something.

Winter taper

In our situation the taper, leading towards the Short Course American Championships, has to be a group taper. I am unable to give the kind of individual attention that I feel is desirable. I do have the opportunity for this in the summer and there is no doubt that it is better. The taper in the final phase of the winter season is a compromise, due to school pressures as well as to facilities. We start about three weeks from the championships, doing less intensive training, giving more rest interval between repeats and beginning to work more specifically for speed and we occasionally cut down on the morning swims. But we usually carry the morning workouts right through to the end of the season—again with less yardage, more stroke technique and pace training during this period. The occasional 'morning off' does help to speed up the recovery from fatigue. However, in the summer leading towards the end of the season major championships we are able to do a much more individual taper, which I will explain in detail in the next chapter.

Following the American Short Course Championships which have been our winter's goal, the senior team usually takes about a ten-day rest period, often completely out of the water. But some swimmers do not like to stay out of the water too long—they lose their 'feel' for the water. I give the swimmers the earliest date I will allow them back in the water and also the latest date for starting again. I then leave each swimmer to decide for himself just when he will return to training.

D: April–September

Beginning in late April or early May our programme is on a twice-a-day basis. And for the swimmer who is out of school by this time the intensity of training really picks up. I find that I must first 'condition' the swimmers to the idea that swimming is almost a full-time commitment. This past year, being a post-Olympic year, I have found it necessary to use a new technique to motivate our swimmers to really become involved with their swimming. Swimming two workouts a day is quite demanding, but when a swimmer is out of school this will still leave him with much time on his hands. So this year I introduced a third workout during the lunch time period. This workout was not held under ideal conditions— we were only able to use one lane in a local swimming pool— but I did feel that the extra yardage was important at this stage and wanted to give the swimmers an extra commitment in the middle of the day, encouraging each swimmer's mind to become swimming-orientated. This was, I found, enough to really involve everyone and to start to eliminate the other distractions that prevent them from being totally dedicated.

But I found that the few swimmers who had only had light workouts during the winter (following the Munich Olympics) needed something extra. So I arranged to swim four workouts a day. We swam these four workouts over a three-week period. During this time the swimmers that were on the programme became totally involved in swimming. It was tough, both physically and mentally. Physically, not only were there the demands of performing in the four workouts, but also the problems of having to get to each workout, in the water and out again, and repeating this four times a day. And in some cases at four different locations in the City. For these swimmers the whole day, from 6.30 a.m. through to 7.30 p.m. was virtually all swimming. I would say that it was probably the most demanding period we have experienced to date.

Once this three-week period was completed I had total commitment from the swimmers who had taken the programme. Leslie was one of those swimmers. After this we went back to three workouts a day for the following month. And then finally down to two workouts a day. And on the last three weeks prior to the Canadian National Championships we went to one workout a day (compulsory) with a second workout optional.

For the individual medley swimmer, such as Leslie, on this heavy number of workouts, I found it best to work on two specific strokes in the first workout, and to concentrate on the other two strokes during the second workout. This way the individual medley swimmer seemed to gain a lot—by having enough time during the day to think about every stroke.

All the individual medley swimmers on this programme did have good results at the Canadian Championships this year—as I illustrated earlier. I feel that it was a success, so no doubt we will use this pattern again.

10

Taper

The taper, which is the gradual decrease in work load and increase in quality swimming prior to a swimming championships or meet, is important and must be understood. Without this understanding all the work you have done throughout the season can be ruined.

There are several types of taper. The type of taper to be used will depend on:
(i)   The type of competition being worked towards.
(ii) The type of event you are wanting to perform well in.
(iii) The importance of the meet itself.

Before the season starts you should have made your plans for the coming year. You must know at what points you really have to bring your swimmers down from endurance training —heavy repeats with lots of yardage—to some level of good competitive times.

The only really long taper will come at the final phase of the year, when you are going towards your major championships event. Prior to that all tapers will be on the small taper concept, where you want to be able to continue the season and so be able to get back into endurance work quickly after your short-term goal has been achieved.

However, it is important to taper to some degree more than once in a season. Because without an adequate taper and rest, you are not really going to be able to evaluate just how well your programme is working for you.

A small taper can be used as a 'rehearsal' prior to the main taper for the end-of-season championships.

Each taper has to be worked out, working backwards on a calendar, counting off the 'X' number of days that you want to taper from the date of the competition.

The range of taper periods are:

1. The short taper—approximately three days.
2. Taper for an important meet, such as Provincial or area championships, but not a major championships. This will be in the region of 7–10 days.
3. Taper for the major championships. This will be anywhere from 10 days to three to four weeks.
   The type of taper for each individual swimmer will depend on:
(i) The events he is training for.
(ii) The duration of the actual competition.
(iii) The number of events the swimmer will be competing in during the competition.
(iv) The amount of work that he has done previously.
(v) His actual attitude towards peaking out and 'going bust' for the one event.

Things to do for:
1. The short taper
(a) Reduce slightly the work-load—allow a little more rest between repeats.
(b) Instead of doing all work swimming circles, do a few short sprints each day. Usually walk-back one-length sprints are pretty good. We are able to get in both the start from a standing position and practise finishing the length well. Maybe swim two or three short one-length sprints, breath-holding. Maybe the last ten minutes of water time should be spent on turns, just to be specific, to emphasize making the turns well.
(c) During the actual practice talk a little bit about the competition itself (low-key mental preparation). Explain who will be there, the sort of times you expect from the opposition and also go over maybe a couple of the better practice swims they have had the last week or two weeks of practice. Aim to have a good goal of trying to beat that particular time. But do not spend too much time on this. If you are going onto about a three-day rest period after a long period of constant work, it is unlikely you are going to get great times out of your swimmers. If you set their minds thinking about real top-class performances at this point, some swimmers could come out a little

disappointed. Particularly if they do not go quite as well as you would have expected. Too much motivation wouldn't be the right angle at this point.

2. Taper for an important event
For the second type of taper—7–10 days—which is to qualify for the National Championships or something of this nature—the following pattern should be followed:
(a) Introduce maybe a couple of team meetings to explain how much work you've put in and how to expect the taper to be most effective over this period.
(b) Realistic goal-setting can now be introduced with some evaluation of the past few weeks of swimming—an indication of what to expect from each swimmer at this point. Try and be fairly realistic in setting these goals. If you set your goals too high the usual result is that a swimmer knowing this is a particularly tough time can become a little too anxious and maybe a little up-tight. And he will strain a little too much in his effort to make the time. However, if you set your goals too low this can very often be interpreted by your swimmers as lack of confidence in them.
(c) Most of this taper would be on a group basis in the work-outs, being geared to expecting best times so far for the season.
(d) A little more time should be spent on warm-ups and loosen-downs following work.
(e) If we are introducing more sprint work with rest, then most of the swimmers expect to be stiff and this requires more mobility and loosening exercises, both on land and in the water. Usually a good way of loosening up swimmers, both physically and mentally, is to have them working in pairs during their normal land training programme, massaging each other. This is a good way of getting a pleasant little bit of relief from the normal monotony and the swimmers normally work very well with a little guidance from the coach or masseur. They usually rub a swimmer down and work in the way they think a massage should be applied to them. Having

pairs of swimmers working together over a period of ten days or so, getting in four or five of these rub-downs, provides a good way of releasing tension and giving a feeling of well-being. (f) At this point some broken swimming should be introduced, where the actual race distance is broken up into sections and specific times are being aimed at. Usually, it is a good point to start working on a time-trial basis. For instance, for the half-way distance of a particular event, practising maybe going out the exact time they would like to be hitting in the actual race. Work a little more towards using the practice as a warm-up rehearsal and after about 45–60 minutes work, make a race-distance effort. The whole thing is simulating what would actually happen at a swim meet. This helps to create the atmosphere of a meet and works well to 'bridge the gap' between the usual training programme and competition itself.

Most swimmers, when they go to the championships they have been working towards, are very conscious of resting and not overdoing anything. And very often they don't do enough warm-up work and are not ready for their race. So the above idea can be very useful.

3. *Taper for the major Championships*
This is the main and final taper of the year, when all the work that has been put in through the season has to 'pay off' with best times.

Although this taper is worked to a certain degree on a team basis, it is necessary to work on a much more individual basis at this point. This requires much daily preparation by the coach—keeping very close records of swimmers' reactions to the work done. Fortunately at this point you have usually already been through two or three fairly long taper periods.

In addition to the things that have already been mentioned, the following points should be noted:
(a) A much more detailed mental preparation should take place. This can be done verbally by the coach, with much confidence-building during workouts. Have group meetings

to discuss things common to the whole group and also individual differences to a certain degree. Set up goals—especially
team goals. There is very little pressure on relay swims and
often lifetime-best performances come under these conditions.
So verbally reinforce the confidence of your team. Written
information is also valuable. Put ideas on your notice board,
distribute hand-outs with details of how to rest, eat and train
during this period. Swimmers need considerable guidance
during this three-week taper period. Weight is often a
problem, with less work and the idea of trying to rest and
conserve energy for the one big effort. Care must be taken to
avoid boredom setting in. Much thought must be given to
motivation. Use all the available pooltime, but take much more
time in setting up workouts. Do lots of timing over distances—
and even at this point, as long as it is used carefully, the idea of
swimming two or three people together on 'fun' activities can
be stimulating.

(b) Start to work out at about the same time you'll be racing
when you go to the Championships. Try and take both a
morning and an evening workout and on some days make an
all-out effort over the race distance on both occasions. This
will give the same kind of experience to be coped with later in
the actual competition. Often a swimmer has to produce his
lifetime-best in the heats to qualify for finals. So to practise
swimming heats and finals is important.

(c) Start working hard on establishing a race pattern and
discussing the type of tactics that may have to be used. It
could be a very simple explanation of a negative type of
splitting in the race to be able to achieve a best-performance.
It could be that in a fairly closely contested race a swimmer
should use the tactics of uneven-pace splitting. But this has
to be practised. If a competitor just decides to try it on the day,
it could upset him as much or more than his opposition.

(d) Try to establish a type of local publicity for the event that
you are going to, so that the swimmers realize the importance
of the event itself. If you have good liaison with the local press
you can make it a non-pressure type of publicity.

(e) Rest as much as possible and establish the idea of sleeping under good conditions in a darkened room and a relaxed atmosphere. If it is noisy outside, add three or so layers of curtains to the window. This type of thing must be looked at carefully.

(f) Practise the type of warm-up to be used in competition many times. Teach the swimmer to understand when the warm-up is sufficient.

Practise 'rule of thumb' warm-up principles:
(i)   If a swimmer is going fast but it is hard work, he is not ready to compete.
(ii) If he is swimming easily but slowly, he is not ready to compete.
(iii) When he is swimming FAST and EASILY (feeling good), then he is ready for his race.

It is necessary to practise warm-ups in workout time to find out just when each swimmer is ready to compete. This will vary with each individual.

(g) The physiotherapist/masseur can be of great assistance during this taper period. I find that while swimmers are actually being massaged they are most receptive to race plans, etc.

(h) Make sure that your team is well equipped for the Championships. Ensure that they have towels, robes, change of suits, etc.

(i) Once you leave the normal workout routine of long-distance repeats and hard training, swimmers often react in quite the opposite way to what you would expect. It is quite common during the first four/five days of the taper period to find that times are slower. And even with more rest between repeats the work seems a little harder. This must be carefully explained to your swimmers—they must understand that this is quite common with other athletes as well as themselves. The change of pace and priorities takes some time to adjust to, but after five or six days times will come down.

(j) Make sure that the team is shaved down completely for the Championships. It is important that for the main meet of the year the swimmers feel good. The value of the shave-down has been proved so many times that coaches and swimmers can use it with confidence. The shave-down will depend on the individual. Many good swimmers like to qualify in the heats without shaving down and then shave for the finals. This gives them that feeling of a 'little bit extra' for the main effort. Some like to half-shave for the heats and make their final shave-down prior to finals. Although a swimmer may have two or three important events to compete in over a five/six day competition period, he is usually keen to perform well in one event in particular. Many swimmers leave their final shave-down until this event, even if it is just the shaving of the arms left until last.

(k) Pre-race meals should be discussed. Each swimmer should be encouraged to do what he has found to be best for him in the past. This has to be a case of 'trial and error' by the individual. The type of diet that makes him feel the best and he believes in most usually turns out to be the answer. There are many recommendations in sports journals on this subject.

(l) Words of encouragement before the race are important. Give each swimmer a final reminder about the most important point to concentrate on during the race. Wait for the swimmer after the race and discuss how he felt about the event. This feed-back can be used to advantage later on in the meet, or even at another competition.

(m) The importance of swimming-down after a race should be stressed, particularly if the swimmer has other races to follow.

General points for consideration

(i) Make early reservations prior to the championships, particularly the major meet of the year. Take a good hotel/motel with adequate meals in the close vicinity of the meet. Make sure that you have good transportation to and from the meet. The location is important—and preferably choose an hotel where there are no other swim teams. This makes for less distractions for your swimmers.

(ii) Arrange for two or three small meets during your taper and use them as quality swims. Providing that swimmers swim 'honestly' and strongly they can be a good indication of how the taper is working at that point. And from this you can decide whether or not to make any adjustments to your programme.

(iii) Once the taper period has started you are working primarily for speed, good stroke mechanics, good starts and turns and pace work. Although these are the main considerations, time should be taken to return to your normal type of workouts every three or four days. This helps to relax the swimmers and maintain their physical condition.

(iv) All in all, it is most important to consider the individual swimmer when planning your taper. Group training can be effective, but every swimmer on your programme will have different needs.

The Taper for the Individual Medley swimmer
The taper for the individual medley competitor will follow the same basic pattern as that used by competitors in other events. The fundamentals apply to all events. But all four strokes must be worked into the taper. I find that it is best to work for two or three days on one stroke, but SOME work should be done on all four strokes. In this way times can be brought down on individual strokes while maintaining the performance in others. Short sprints should be swum on the four strokes every day.

Turning in I.M. events is vital, particularly picking up quickly after a turn into the new stroke. Much time has to be spent on turn practices during workouts—far more time than is necessary for a one-stroke race. This subject is discussed and explained in detail in Chapter 13, 'Turns and Stroke Transitions'.

Bruce Robertson became the first Dolphin to win the title of World Champion, when he won the 100 metres butterfly at the 1973 World Aquatic Games in Belgrade. Here he is seen receiving his gold medal from Dr. H. W. Henning, President of FINA.

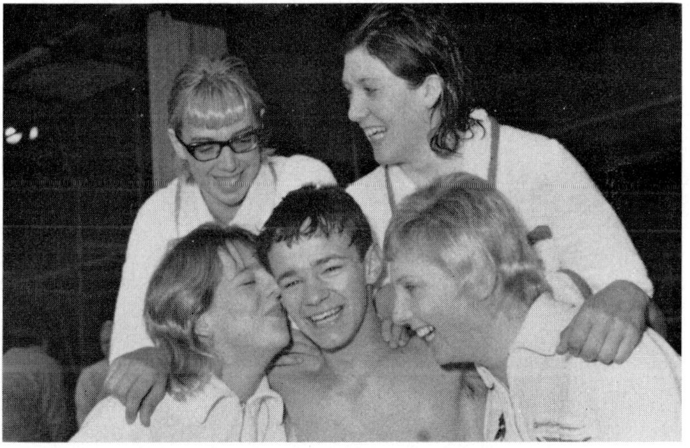

'This programme has been responsible for producing a large number of successful individual medley swimmers.' Alan Kimber, the author's first outstanding I.M. swimmer, is seen here receiving congratulations from England's star medley relay team—left to right: Linda Ludgrove, Stella Mitchell, Elizabeth Long, Judy Gegan.

Butterfly is the lead-off stroke of the I.M. Jennifer McHugh, Canadian 200 metres Butterfly Champion demonstrates her powerful stroke. Exercises for each phase of the stroke are given in the book.

Season-long individual daily workout plan (Leslie Cliff)

I asked Leslie to compile a comprehensive series of workouts that she has swum and enjoyed. She has given sessions for both summer and winter and has included stroke workouts, endurance training and quality work, plus the type of programme that we work on during taper periods.

As I believe it is important to keep workouts interesting, I also asked her to include her favourite workouts.

Typical Weeks
September–Christmas
(training in a 32 yard pool)

Monday	*7:00–8:00 a.m.* 3,850 yards
5,850 yards	400 swim
	200 kick
	6 × 2 @ 60
	1,650 pull—half free, half back
	3 × 400 free @ 6:00
	6:20–7:00 p.m. 2,000 yards
	6 × 2 kick @ 1:15
	200 s.a. fly
	10 × 2 fly @ 1:30
	4 × 200 free kick @ 4:00
Tuesday	*7:00–8:00 a.m.* 2,800 yards
4,800 yards	400 swim
	400 kick
	400 pull
	6 × 2 free @ 60
	4 × 300 @ 5:00 100 back pull, 100 breast pull, 100 free pull

6:20–7:00 p.m.   2,000 yards
6 × 2 kick @ 1:15
6 × 2 free @ 55 with paddles
5 × 200 breast kick @ 4:00
3 × 2 breast @ 1:30

Wednesday	no morning swimming
3,600 yards	*7:00–8:00 p.m.*

6 × 2 kick @ 1:15
6 × 2 free @ 55
6 × 2 free @ 50
10 × 200 free @ 2:30
200 kick
3 × 2 free @ 1:30

Thursday	*7:00–8:00 a.m.* 2,600 yards
4,600 yards	400 kick

6 × 2 free @ 60
200 s.a. fly
200 fly kick
8 × 150 fly @ 3:00
200 free easy
6:20–7:00 p.m.   2,000 yards
6 × 2 kick @ 1:15
6 × 2 back @ 1:15
200 back kick
8 × 100 back @ 1:45
100 easy
100 back hard

Friday	no swimming in the morning
3,400 yards	*7:00–8:00 p.m.*

6 × 2 kick @ 1:15
6 × 2 free @ 55
16 × 2 back pull @ 1:10
16 × 2 back @ 1:10
200 kick
3 × 2 free @ 1:30   (descending)
3 × 2 free @ 2:00   (descending)

Saturday	no swimming

Sunday   *9:00–11:00 a.m.*
4,700 yards   800 swim
                  800 kick
                  800 pull
                  400 breaststroke   stretching
                  400 breaststroke kick
                  8 × 2 free @ 55
                  5 × 200 breaststroke @ 4:00   (descending)

Total Yardage for the Week—26,950 yards

*Typical Week—Intensive Training—
Winter 1973*

Monday   *7:00–8:30 a.m.*   4,840 yards
8,440 yards   400 swim
                  400 kick
                  400 pull
                  6 × 2 free @ 55
                  4 × 400 @ 6:30   two back pull, one back pull with
                                   paddles, one full stroke back
                                   hard
                  400 pull breast
                  400 breast kick
                  400 breast
                  200 free easy
                  200 free hard
                  5:40–7:00 p.m.   3,600 yards
                  6 × 2 kick @ 1:15
                  6 × 2 free @ 55
                  5 × 200 kick @ 3:30
                  4 × 200 free @ 3:30 with paddles
                  6 × 2 back pull with paddles @ 1:15
                  6 × 2 back kick @ 1:30
                  3 × 2 back @ 2:00

Tuesday   *7:00–8:30 a.m.*   5,440 yards
8,440 yards   400 swim
                  400 kick
                  400 pull
                  400 swim
                  6 × 2 free @ 55

10 × 200 back @ 3:00
200 fly kick
200 single arm fly
400 dive fly
400 hard fly
200 easy
5:40–7:00 p.m.   3,000 yards
6 × 2 kick @ 1:15
6 × 2 free @ 55
5 × 200 fly kick @ 3:30
6 × 2 free @ 50
4 × 200 free   lots of rest   hard

Wednesday   *7:00–8:30 a.m.*   5,440 yards
10,480 yards   200 swim
200 kick
200 pull
200 swim
880 back pull
6 × 2 free @ 55
800 stroke work back
3 × 440 back @ 7:00
440 easy free
400 free pull
400 free hard
6:00–8:00 p.m.   5,040 yards
6 × 2 kick @ 1:15
6 × 2 free pull @ 1:10
5 × 200 kick @ 3:45
3 × 2 back—breast @ 1:10
5 × 200 free pull @ 3:30
3 × 2 breast—free @ 1:10
4 × 200 free @ 5:00
400 easy kick
440 breast
3 × 2 breast @ 2:00

Thursday   no swimming in the morning
2,940 yards   *5:40–7:00 p.m.*   2,940 yards
6 × 2 kick @ 1:15
6 × 2 @ 1:15 back—breast
400 back kick

6 × 2 @ 1:15 breast—free, 4 × 100 back @ 2:00
1 × 2 back hard, 4 × 100 @ 2:00 easy, 1 × 100
back hard
200 single arm fly, 200 dive fly

Friday
8,320 yards

7:00–8:30 a.m.   4,320 yards
200 swim
400 kick
1,200 swim, 400 s.a. fly, 400 s.a. back, 400 pull
breast
880 free pull
3 × 440 free @ 7:00
400 fly hard
1 × 2 easy
6:00–8:00 p.m.   4,000 yards
400 kick
6 × 2 @ 1:10 back—breast
3 × 200 back kick @ 4:00
6 × 2 @ 1:15 breast—free
7 × 200 free @ 3:00
400 fly kick
1 × 200 free hard
1 × 200 easy

Saturday
2,700 yards

6:30–7:30 p.m.
200 swim
400 kick
400 pull
6 × 2 breast @ 1:15
400 s.a. fly
6 × 1 fly @ 35
1 × 2 easy
6 × 1 fly @ 30
200 easy
100 fly   hard, 100 easy
1 × 1 free   hard

Sunday
4,500 yards

11:00 a.m.–1:00 p.m.
6 × 2 fly kick @ 1:15
6 × 2 fly—back @ 1:10
6 × 2 breast—free @ 1:15
3 × 880 free @ 14:00

6 × 2 back @ 2:00
150 single arm fly
1 × 2 fly   hard

Total Yardage for the Week—45,820 yards

Typical Week—Intensive Training—Summer

Monday   *10:00–11:30 a.m.*   5,060 yards
7,920 yards+ (55 yards pool)
5,400 metres   440 kick
8 × 55 free @ 55
8 × 55 free @ 50
8 × 55 free @ 45
880 back   last 440 hard
440 I.M. kick
5 × 200 I.M. @ 3:30
880 with 2 singles hard
1:30–2:30 p.m.   2,860 yards
(55 yards pool)
440 swim
8 × 220 free @ 3:30
4 × 110 breast @ 2:00   last 25 hard
4 × 55 breast @ 1:15   2 hard
5:30–7:00 p.m.   5,400 metres
(25 metre pool)
6 × 50 kick @ 60
8 × 50 free pull @ 55
4 × 100 breast kick @ 2:00
6 × 2 free @ 45
20 × 200 back @ 3:00

Tuesday   *7:30–9:00 a.m.*   5,740 yards
9,700 yards+ (32 yard pool)
4,800 metres   4 × 2 kick @ 1:15
4 × 2 free @ 55
4 × 100 fly kick @ 1:45
8 × 220 back pull @ 3:30
4 × 220 back @ 3:30
8 × 220 free pull @ 3:00
2 × 220 free one easy one hard

1:30–2:45 p.m.   3,960 yards
(55 yard pool)
440 swim
4 × 55 free @ 50
5 × 440 free @ 5:30
5 × 220 breast @ 5:00   (descending)

5:00–7:00 p.m.   4,800 metres
(25 metre pool)
8 × 50 fly kick @ 1:10
16 × 2 back pull @ 60
4 × 100 back kick @ 2:15
3 × 2 back @ 1:30
12 × 100 free pull @ 1:45
3 × 100 free @ 3:00
30 × 2 fly @ 60
1 × 2 fly hard

Wednesday   *7:30–9:00 a.m.*   3,960 yards
6,930 yards+ (32 yard pool)
7,100 metres 400 kick
6 × 2 free @ 55
8 × 100 breast @ 2:00
5 × 200 breast kick @ 4:00
440 breast pull
1 × 220 breast pull hard
3 × 220 breast @ 5:00

1:30–2:30 p.m.   2,970 yards
(55 yard pool)
440 single arm fly
440 single arm back and double arm back
440 free
10 × 1 free @ 60
10 × 110 @ 2:00   single arm up—full stroke
                          down

5:00–7:00 p.m.   7,100 metres
(25 metre pool)
6 × 2 kick @ 60
8 × 2 free @ 50
16 × 400 free @ 6:00

Thursday   *7:30–9:00 a.m.*   4,270 yards
6,360 yards+   (32 yard pool)
5,600 metres   4 × 2 kick @ 1:10
6 × 2 free @ 55
10 × 100 breast kick @ 2:00
400 breast easy
4 × 220 back kick @ 5:00
400 breast easy
440 free kick hard
440 swim easy
1 × 2 free kick hard

1:30–2:30 p.m.   2,090 yards
(55 yard pool)
220 swim
330 single arm fly
5 × 220 fly @ 5:00
220 easy
4 × 55 fly @ 2:00

5:00–7:00 p.m.   5,600 metres
(25 metre pool)
8 × 2 kick @ 60
30 × 2 free pull @ 55
30 × 2 free @ 55
4 × 2 free kick @ 60
16 × 2 back pull @ 60
4 × 100 back @ 2:00 easy
4 × 100 back @ 1:45 hard
4 × 100 back @ 1:30 hard

Friday   *7:30–9:00 a.m.*   4,050 yards
12,370 yards   (32 yard pool)
400 fly kick
6 × 2 free @ 55
200 back kick
10 × 220 back @ 3:30
250 fly kick
12 × 2 fly @ 1:30

10:30–11:30 a.m.   2,640 yards
(55 yard pool)
440 swim

220 kick
8 × 55 free @ 50
10 × 110 fly @ 2:15
8 × 55 fly @ 1:15

1:30–2:30 p.m.   2,420 yards
(55 yard pool)
220 swim
30 × 55 breast @ 60
4 × 110 breast   last 25 hard
2 × 55   one easy   one hard

6:30–8:00 p.m.   3,260 yards
(32 yard pool)
8 × 2 kick @ 60
6 × 2 free @ 55
4 × 100 free kick @ 2:00
3 × 2 free @ 60
4 × 100 breast kick @ 2:00
8 × 2 breast pull @ 1:15
3 × 2 breast @ 2:00 (descending)
3 × 2 breast @ 2:00 (descending)
12 × 1 free @ 45
1 × 2 free   hard

Saturday
6,600 yards

9:00–11:00 a.m.
(55 yard pool)
220 swim
4 × 55 free @ 55
4 × 55 free @ 50
4 × 55 back @ 40
5 × 110 free @ 2:00   last 25 hard
10 × 220 free @ 2:40
4 × 55 breast @ 60
110 single arm fly
12 × 220 back @ 3:30

Sunday   no swimming

Total Yardage for the Week—49,880 yards +
22,900 metres

Taper period (April–September)

July 13 (*prior to* *National* *Champion-* *ships*)	(50 metre pool) 400 swim 200 kick 10 × 1 free @ 1:30 out easy, back hard: 31.6 30.5 30.6 31.6 29.0 200 easy 8 × 1 back @ 1:30 out easy, back hard: 34.3 33.7 33.1 33.9 200 easy 4 × 1 fly from dive @ 2:00—33.2 31.8 30.8 31.5
July 17	(50 metre pool) 3 × 100 back kick 2:00 1:53 1:51 2 × 100 back pull 1:34 1:27 2 × 400 free @ 6:30—5:07 4:41 3 × 200 free @ 4:00—2:35 2:25 2:20 4 × 100 breast @ 3:00—1:35 1:30 1:28 1:24 2 × 50 fly 34.00 34.00
August 17 (*prior to* *World* *Aquatic* *Champion-* *ships*)	(50 metre pool) 400 swim 200 fly stroke work 200 back stroke work 200 breast stroke work 3 × 400 I.M. 5:39 @ 8.00 5:25 @ 10.00 5:08 1 × 100 free easy 3 × 100 fly @ 2:30—1:20 1:20 1:20
August 23	(50 metre pool) 400 swim 400 kick 16 × 1 I.M. fly @ 60 back @ 60 breast @ 1:15 free @ 60 200 easy 200 I.M. 2:28.9 200 fly kick easy 2 × 50 fly kick hard 38.9 38.9

Favourite Workouts

(*1*) *Endur-* *ance* *Workout* 5,500 metres	400 swim (anything) 8 × 50 kick @ 1:05 16 × 50 free @ 55 8 × 400 back @ 7:00 (descending but not starting off slow) 200 kick 10 × 50 free @ 60 up easy, down hard
(*2*) *Stroke* *Workout* (breaststroke)	400 swim (anything) 400 kick breaststroke (arms behind back) 400 breaststroke pull 8 × 50 free @ 60 400 breaststroke two kicks to one pull two pulls to one kick stretching 5 × 200 breaststroke (descending, starting off slow, only really working the last one)
(*3*) *Quality* *Workout* (trying to get a fast 50 fly)	400 swim 400 kick fly 8 × 50 free @ 55 400–800 stroke work—single arm, dive stroke, long stroke 4 × 50 fly @ 2:30 not hard—trying to feel good about 3 × 50 with lots of rest—or more—until you have gone as fast as you can go.

12

Land conditioning exercises

Much of our swimming conditioning is done in the water through a balanced programme which includes both endurance and speed swimming. But we do a variety of land conditioning exercises as well.

Land work is often neglected for several reasons. Either a lack of knowledge on the part of the coach, lack of facilities or lack of time. But the three aspects of physical conditioning required for good swimming performance—STRENGTH, ENDURANCE and FLEXIBILITY—can be improved more quickly if work in the water is supplemented with land-work. GENERAL FITNESS, too, is a natural by-product of a well-constructed land conditioning programme, as is speed.

1. General fitness
This is a necessary base on which to build specific fitness in a swimmer. Swimming is a tough sport, so general fitness is essential if the body is to stand up to the various stresses placed on it, both in training and in competition.

2. Strength
Lack of strength will eventually limit a swimmer's performance. The young swimmer often compensates for a lack of strength with a high level of endurance and/or stroke technique. The muscles used in swimming must be strong to accept the heavy work load. But it is important that the programme is designed to strengthen the muscles that are used for propulsion in swimming and that the exercises relate to the movements used in the swimming strokes. A body-building programme, for instance, is not suitable.

Basically, strength can best be improved by doing high-resistance exercises with low repetitions.

3. Endurance
It is essential that endurance is built up, both in the muscular and circulo-respiratory systems. Local muscular endurance is necessary when swimming a particular stroke, with continuous use of the same muscles throughout a race. Good circulo-respiratory efficiency allows these muscle groups to work strongly and consistently over long periods. Middle and long distance swimmers obviously need high endurance. And as I encourage my individual medley swimmers and potential I.M. swimmers to swim as many events as possible in a meet, endurance work is important for them, too.

Generally, high repetitions of exercises involving low resistance are used for increasing endurance—although there is a certain amount of overlap and carry-over in both strength and endurance work.

The exercises we use to improve endurance include:
(a) Intensive sprinting (both in the water and running).
(b) Kicking drills in the water.
(c) Endurance running.
(d) Weight training for local muscular endurance.
(e) Work with pulleys.
(f) Circuit training.

Flexibility
Mobility of the joints is essential for the swimmer to perform the correct stroke movements. Suppleness and strength in the joints and surrounding areas can best be improved by doing stretching exercises and basic weight training.

Some exercises to improve flexibility are:
 1. High leg swings backwards and forwards, using support.
 2. Hurdle stretching—head to knee.
 3. Arm circles.
 4. Toe-touching, palms flat, legs straight.
 5. Squat jumps—arched back.
 6. Ankle manipulation, sitting down and working with both hands.

7. Arm-pulls—swinging arms backwards at shoulder level as far as possible, alternately bent and straight.
8. 'Dislocations' on rings, ropes or bars.
9. Cycling, making as large circles as possible.
10. High-kicking—straight leg up above head.

Points to consider when planning a land conditioning programme
(a) Individual swimmers will have different degrees of strength, endurance and flexibility. Therefore, their capabilities and training needs must be taken into account when setting tasks.
(b) The amount and type of landwork will depend on water time and facilities. Water time is valuable, but some land work should be fitted in at other times. Those clubs who have limited swimming time can do much to improve the fitness of the team by using a well-balanced land conditioning programme. Lack of facilities should never be a deterent, there are many exercises which require no apparatus and little space.
(c) Work on the land should be related to swimming.
(d) Use a careful build-up with young swimmers and proper progressions. Keep the programme interesting, fast-moving and challenging.

Land conditioning exercises for swimmers
There are numerous exercises in each category which can be used to improve those physical qualities essential in competitive swimming—STRENGTH, ENDURANCE, FLEXIBILITY and GENERAL FITNESS. The following pages include a selection of those exercises I have found to be particularly suitable and beneficial. They fall under the following headings.
A. Calisthenics
B. Weight training
C. Pulleys
D. Isometrics
E. Circuit training
F. Exergenie (cord work)

A. Calisthenics

This group includes exercises without apparatus. These are especially valuable for those clubs which have restricted space or facilities. They are used to maintain GENERAL BODY FITNESS and FLEXIBILITY. STRENGTH and EN-DURANCE can also be improved. In these exercises the swimmer's own body weight is the resistance being worked against.

1. Press-Ups

Starting position: Hands on the floor, shoulder-width apart, arms fully extended, toes curled under. The whole body, including the seat, should be in line.

The exercise: Bend the elbows and lower the chin so that it is just off the floor. Extend the arms and return to the starting position.

Points to stress:
(i)   The hands should be directly under the shoulders.
(ii) The whole body remains straight throughout the exercise —avoid arching the back or sticking the seat out.
(iii) The arms do all the work.
(iv) Only the hands and toes contact the floor.

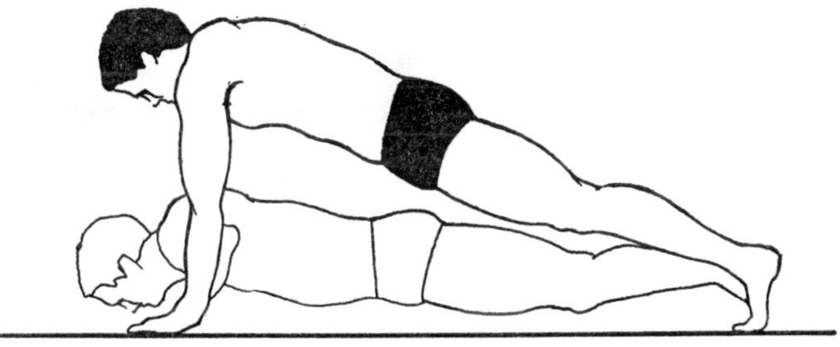

Fig. 1. Press-ups.

Variations:
(a)   Hands raised, on a bench.
(b)   Feet raised, on a bench.
(c)   With a clap.

97

2. Sit-ups/Trunk Curls

Starting position: (as illustrated in fig. 2(a)). Lie on back, body extended, hands resting on thighs. Feet may be held or fixed.

The exercise: Slide hands forward to knees, curling trunk. Return to starting position.

Points to stress:

(i)   The movement is started by bending the head forward.

(ii) The whole exercise should be performed rhythmically and without resting in any position.

(iii) Keep the legs straight all the time and the feet on the floor.

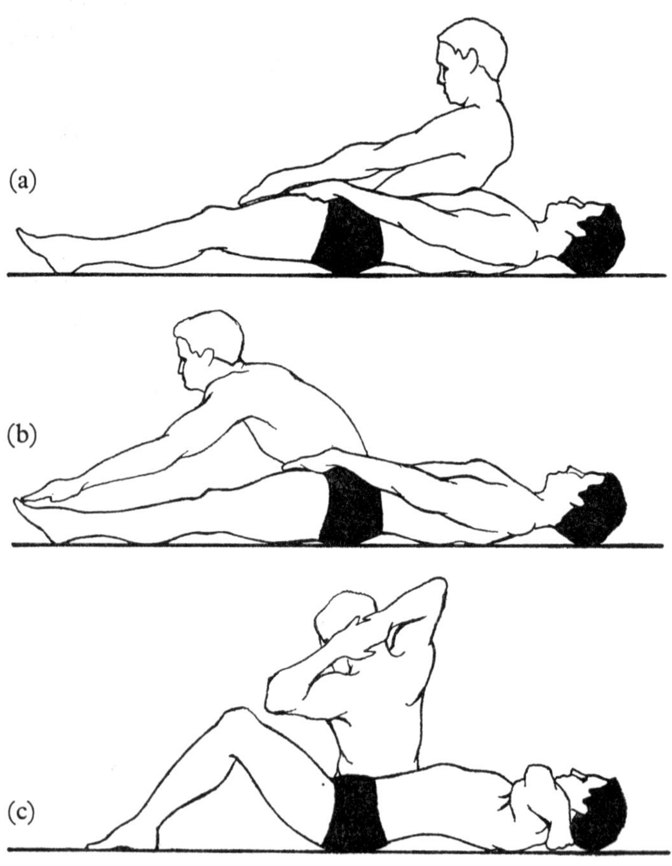

Fig. 2. Sit-ups.

Here Leslie Cliff is seen swimming the breaststroke leg, which is the third leg of the I.M. It is so different from the other strokes and can be either a rest or a drag, depending on how well it is swum. Efficiency is important and swimmers tend to be either natural or impossible breaststrokers. Drills for the stroke are given in the book.

Land conditioning is a valuable part of any swimming programme. David Haller, ex-Olympic sprinter, working out.

Mobility of the joints is essential for the swimmer to perform the correct stroke work. Here a group of young swimmers work for flexibility.

Variations:

(b) Sit-ups to toes (as illustrated).

(c) Sit-ups with bent knees, bring alternate elbow to opposite knee.

3. Head and Chest Raises

Starting position: Lie on stomach, hands clasped behind neck, head down, heels tucked under bench (optional), legs extended.

The exercise: Arch the back by lifting the chest as far off the grounds as possible. Return to starting position.

Points to stress:

(i) Lift the chest as high as possible from the ground.

(ii) LOWER body to starting position, don't 'flop'.

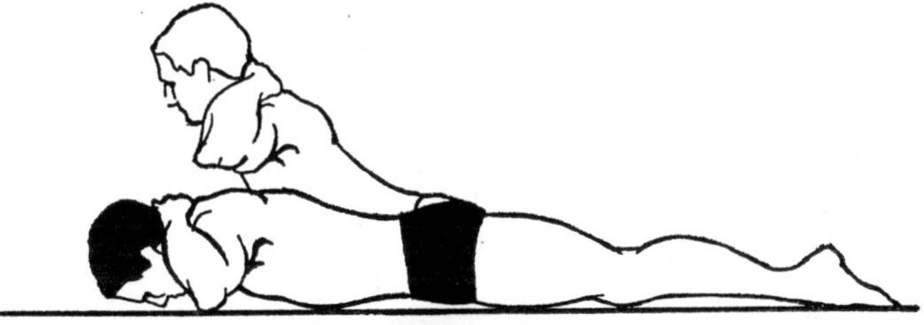

Fig. 3. Head and chest raises.

Variations:

(a) $\frac{1}{2}$-twist to left before lowering body to the ground, followed by $\frac{1}{2}$-twist to the right.

(b) $\frac{1}{2}$-twist to the left and right before lowering body to the ground.

4. Squats

Starting position: Full squat (as illustrated). Feet shoulder-width apart, back straight, hands clasped behind head.

The exercise: Slowly bend the knees and lower the body into the full-squat position, knees fully bent. Straighten legs and return to starting position.

Points to stress:
(i) Pull the elbows back to keep the back as straight as possible.
(ii) To use this as a stretching exercise for the posterior muscles of the lower leg, keep the heels on the ground throughout the exercise. The heels *may* be raised off the ground as the full-squat position is reached.

Fig. 4. Squats.

Variations:
(a) As described, except the knees are only half-bent (angle of more than 90° at knees). This is a half-squat.

5. Squat Thrusts

Starting position: Crouch position, hands outside and just in front of feet.

The exercise: Supporting the body with the hands, thrust the legs backwards to an extended, straight body position. Jump back to starting position.

Points to stress:
(i) Keep the hands under shoulders.
(ii) Emphasize a strong thrust-back of the legs.

Fig. 5. Squat thrusts.

Variations:
(a) Burpee: from a standing position drop down into crouch. Thrust the legs backwards as in a squat thrust and jump back to crouch. Return to standing.
(b) Burpee—springing as high into the air as possible instead of standing in erect position.

6. Squat Jumps

Starting position: Crouch position, arms outside legs, fingers touching the floor.

The exercise: Thrust strongly from the floor using the feet. Spring in a fully-extended arched-back position as high into the air as possible. Land back in the starting position.

Points to stress:

(i) Touching the floor with the fingers aids balance.
(ii) Height in the jump is important.
(iii) A full crouch position should be assumed after the jump.

Fig. 6. Squat jumps.

Variations:

(a) As above, but with straight back in the jump.
(b) Star-jump in the air.

7. Back Arches

Starting position: Lie face-down in extended position, arms above the head.

The exercise: Raise the head and arms and the legs as far off the ground as possible arching the back. Return to starting position.

Points to stress:

(i)   Balance the body on the hips.
(ii) The exercise should be performed rhythmically and continuously.
(iii) Raise the head and feet as far off the ground as possible.

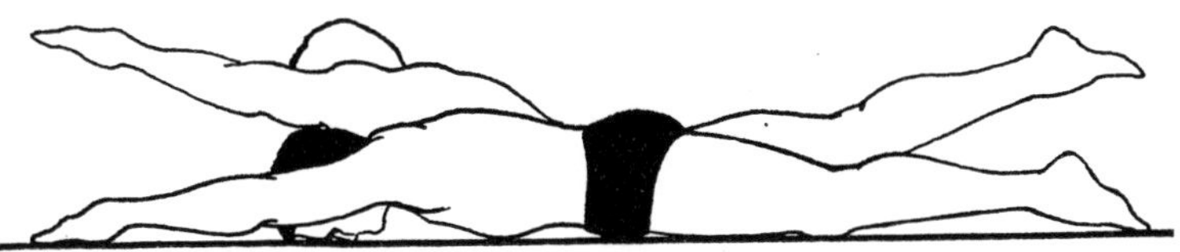

Fig. 7. Back arches.

Variations:

(a)   Raise one arm and the opposite leg simultaneously.
(b)   As described, but with arms down by the sides.

B. Weight training

The main purpose of weight training in a swimming land conditioning programme is to strengthen the muscles used in specific strokes. I have included those which I have found to be useful, showing exercises for arms, legs and trunk.

We do very little weight training during the year, but work hard with weights during our Xmas Workshop.

1. Half-Squats

Starting position: Stand erect, weights balanced evenly with the bar behind the neck and resting on the shoulders. Feet shoulder-width apart, heels on the floor, body balanced.

The exercise: Lower the body to a semi-crouch position. Straighten the legs to return to standing.

Points to stress:
(i)   Keep the back straight throughout the exercise.
(ii) Look straight ahead.
(iii) The legs do all the work.

Fig. 8. Half squats.

2. Dead Lift

Starting position: Crouch position, feet hip-width apart, back straight, toes under the bar, weight evenly balanced, chest forward. Pronated grip, eyes looking upwards and ahead.

The exercise: Lift the weight by straightening the knees and hips. Rise to an erect position, holding the bar across the thighs. Return to starting position.

Points to stress:
(i)   Keep back straight throughout.
(ii) Arms are extended throughout.
(iii) The legs and hips do the work.
(iv) When lifting heavy weights, correct technique is very important.

Fig. 9. Dead lift.

3. Heel Raises

Starting position: Stand erect, feet a few inches apart, toes on a slightly raised surface (one inch or so), bar resting on shoulders.

The exercise: Raise heels as high off the floor as possible, then lower as far below raised surface as possible.

Points to stress:
(i)   Remain erect throughout the exercise.
(ii) Balance carefully on the toes to retain balance—do not lean either forwards or backwards.
(iii) The position of the feet can be varied: turned out slightly (breaststroke); turned inwards slightly (crawl); straight (butterfly).

Fig. 10. Heel raises.

4. Astride Jumps

Starting position: Stand erect on bench, holding dumb-bells with the pronated grip, arms extended.

The exercise: Jump from the bench onto the floor (astride jump) and then back onto the bench.

Points to stress:
(i)   Fast, rhythmical movement.
(ii) Hold head steady and look straight ahead.
(iii) Hold dumb-bells firmly and close to the thighs.

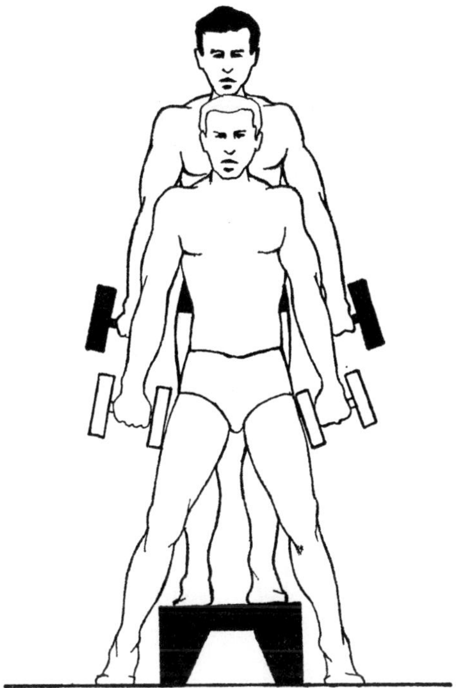

Fig. 11. Astride jumps.

5. Shoulder Presses

Starting position: Rest bar on shoulders, hands just outside the shoulder line (pronated grip), weight evenly balanced with feet shoulder-width apart, body erect.

The exercise: Press the bar upwards from behind the neck until the arms are fully extended. Lower the bar slowly to the shoulder rest position.

Points to stress:
(i)   Focus gaze straight ahead.
(ii) Body should be erect with the chest out.
(iii) Bar should be directly above the shoulders throughout the movement.

Fig. 12. Presses.

6. *Pull Backs*

Starting position: Stand erect with the bar-bell held behind the body and resting against the backs of the thighs. Arms extended, palms of the hands facing backwards.
The exercise: Raise the bar-bell upwards and backwards as far as possible, keeping the arms straight, the elbows locked. Lower the weight to the starting position.

Points to stress:

(i)   Keep body erect and balanced throughout the movement.

Fig. 13. Pull backs.

Variations:

(a)   As described, but bent forward at the waist, the trunk
parallel to the floor. The head should be in line with the
trunk, face to the floor, for this exercise.

7. Rowing

Starting position: Bend forward at the waist and hold the bar
at knee level with pronated grip, hands just outside shoulders.
Stand with feet hip-width apart, legs straight and head in line
with trunk.

The exercise: From this position, draw the bar up to the chest by flexing the arms. Lower to starting position.

Points to stress:
(i)   Keep the back straight throughout.
(ii)   The only movement is in the shoulders and the elbow joints.
(iii)   Look at the floor directly ahead.
(iv)   Bar should be lowered with control, not dropped.
(v)   Elbows should be higher than hands in the lift position.

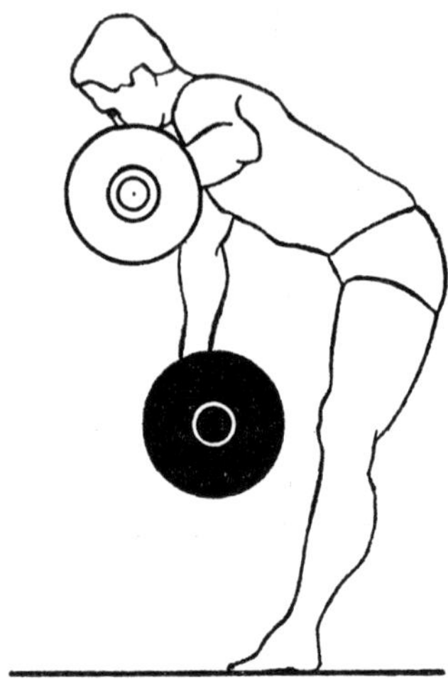

Fig. 14. Rowing.

Variations:
(a)   Rowing in an upright position. As above, but the body is held perfectly erect and the movement begins with the bar held in the thigh-rest position.

8. Wrist Rolling

(using disc-weight attached to a bar with $4\frac{1}{2}$ ft cord).

Starting position: Stand erect holding bar at waist level with pronated grip, the weight just resting on the floor.

The exercise: Roll the bar with the wrists, gradually raising the weight from the floor by rolling it around the bar.

Points to stress:
(i)   Only the arms and wrists do the work.

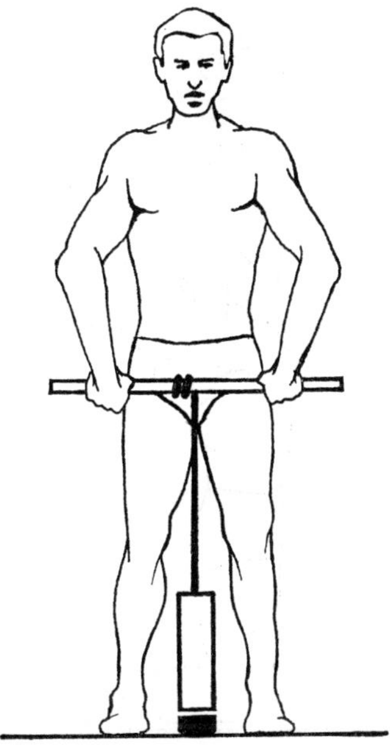

Fig. 15. Wrist rolling.

9. Triceps Curls

Starting position: Kneel down, legs shoulder-width apart, body erect. Hold the dumb-bells/bar-bell overhead, arms fully extended.

The exercise: Lower the weight very slowly behind the back of the neck as far as possible. Return to starting position.

Points to stress:

(i)   Body should be perfectly balanced.

(ii) When dumb-bells/bar-bell are at lowest point behind neck, the elbows should be close to the ears and pointing upwards.

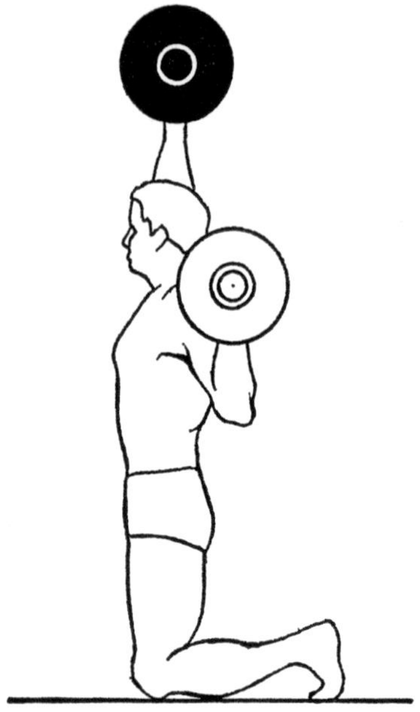

Fig. 16. Triceps curls.

Variations:

(a) As described, standing in an erect position.

10. Straight-Arm Pullovers

Starting position: Lie on back in supine position, feet on the floor and hooked around bench legs. Rest head on bench and extend arms backwards to grip bar on the floor with a pronated grip.

The exercise: Lift the weight in an arc from the floor with straight arms to above the shoulder line. Slowly lower the weight back to the floor.

Points to stress:
(i)   Arms remain straight throughout the exercise.
(ii) Lower the weight to the floor with control—do not drop it.
(iii) Keep lower back in contact with the bench throughout.

Fig. 17. Straight-arm pullovers.

Variations:

(a)   As above, but allowing the arms to bend, shortening the lever to pull through to the extended position above the head.

11. *Trunk Curls*

Starting position: Lie on the floor in the supine position. Fix the feet and extend the body with a weight held behind the head.

The exercise: Pull forward to touch the knees with the elbows. Lower body back to starting position.

Points to stress:

(i)   The movement is started by curling the neck forward.
(ii) Knees may either be straight or slightly bent.

Fig. 18. Trunk curls.

Variations:

(a)   As above, on an inclined bench, feet held with strap.
(b)   As above, twisting the body to touch alternate elbows to opposite knees.

12. Back Lifts

Starting position: Lie across bench, feet held by partner, body bent over at the waist, elbows on the floor, clasping weight.

The exercise: Lift the body upwards from the waist, trying to get the chest as high as possible above the bench. Lower slowly to starting position.

Points to stress:

(i)   Pull the chin in towards the chest.
(ii)   Keep shoulders square and pull the elbows up and out.
(iii) Lower the body to starting position, do not 'drop'.

Lack of strengh will eventually limit a swimmer's performance, so this side of training should not be neglected.

Judy Wright, Canadian Recordholder in 100 yards freestyle demonstrates use of the exer-genie cord machine.

There are many styles of racing start effectively used by top swimmers. This is demonstrated by this photo of the start of the I.M. final at the World Aquatic Games in Belgrade.

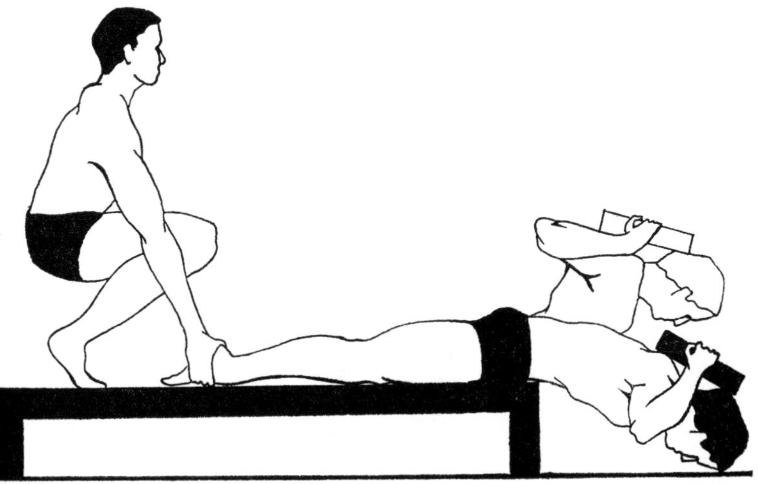

Fig. 19. Back lifts.

C. Pulley weights

We use our own home-made pulleys, which are a permanent fixture. They are just a simple 'lat' machine consisting of heavy ropes running over two sets of rollers mounted overhead.

Movements similar to those used in swimming strokes can be used with pulleys. Both isometric and isotonic work can be done. And work on both the single and double latissimus pulley systems is good for developing specific muscular strength.

The principle of exercise programming is similar to that used in weight training for swimming.

The diagrams (figs. 20 and 21) illustrate work on both single and double pulley systems.

Fig. 20. Pulley weights (single).

D. Isometrics

The methods of training for strength that I have described so far have been those involving ISOTONIC muscle contraction—that is where the muscle actually lengthens and shortens during exercise. ISOMETRIC exercises—where the muscle remains virtually the same length throughout the exercise, whilst working against a resistance—can also be used to build up strength.

Again, this type of exercise is useful for those clubs which

Fig. 21. Pulley weights (double).

have limited facilities and equipment, as all that is required is a partner or a fixed object, such as a wall.

A coach can very easily devise his own programme, using exercises involving pulling or pushing against fixed objects.

There are several reasons for considering the use of isometric exercises in the programme. These are:

(i) The exercises can be done anywhere and at any time.

(ii) There is virtually no muscular fatigue or stress on the

circulo-respiratory system after exercise, which makes it possible to use these exercises even before a heavy workout.
(iii) Muscles can be worked without any movement of the joint—so this can be one way of maintaining strength during injury.
(iv) Actual stroke mechanics can be practised using the isometric principle.

Isometric work can be used as a variation to the programme, but should never be used as a substitute for weight training and other isotonic work.

E. Circuit training

Circuit training is a valuable inclusion in the land conditioning programme, as it can be adapted to cater for just about every component of fitness. Basically, it was designed to improve endurance and general fitness, but can also be used for work on flexibility, strength and speed.

When planning a circuit programme the coach should always have in mind:
(a) The individual differences and needs of each swimmer.
(b) The progressive overload principle—both to make his programme effective and to guard against strain and injury. This can be applied by either gradually increasing the workload, increasing the number of repetitions or decreasing the rest interval.
(c) Have clear in his mind just what he is aiming to achieve from his circuit—whether it is work for flexibility, endurance, strength or just general conditioning.
Circuits can be varied in a number of ways:
(i) The number of stations to be worked. This can vary from three or four up to twelve or so. This will depend upon numbers of swimmers and the amount of space available. The diagram shows an eight-station circuit pattern.
(ii) The type of work being done.
(iii) The TYPE of circuit. These can include:
(a) Circuit without apparatus.
(b) Circuit using simple apparatus (benches, ropes, etc.).

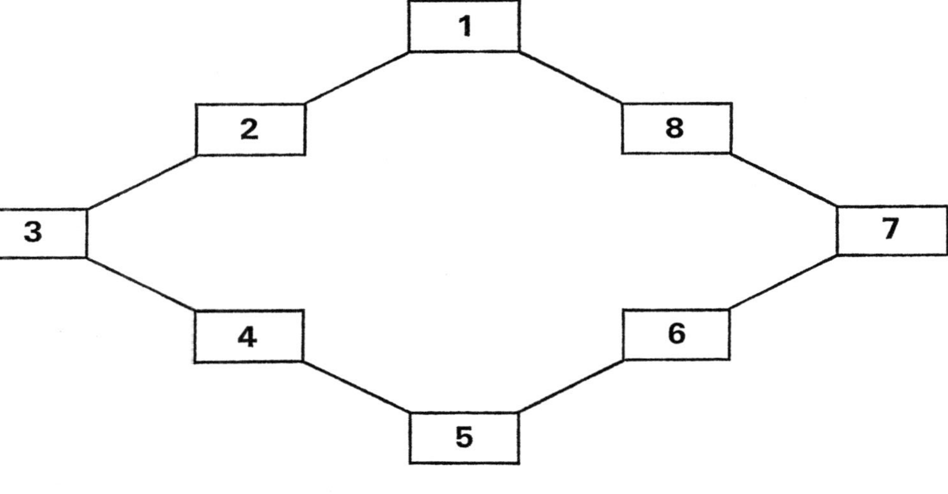

Fig. 22. Diagram of an eight station circuit.

(c) Circuit with weights.
(d) Mixed circuit—including any of (a), (b), or (c).
(e) Circuit using exer-genie (discussed in Section F).
The type of circuit I use with my swimmers varies according to what I am trying to achieve at a particular time. But I do make sure that all parts of the body are exercised, both in isolation and together. In this way the various muscle groups have time to recover between stations.

An eight-station mixed circuit (as illustrated) could include:
1. Dead lifts—weights (legs).
2. Press-ups (arms).
3. Back arches (back and abdominal muscles).
4. Squat jumps (whole body).
5. Astride jumps—bench (legs).
6. Pull-backs (arms).
7. Trunk curls (back/abdominals).
8. Burpees (whole body).

F. Exer-genie

Exer-genie work is particularly good for girls—they achieve the same results and often prefer to use this instead of weights. This piece of equipment can either be used separately or it can be used in a circuit.

For a comprehensive selection of Land Conditioning Exercises for Swimming, refer to the following books:
1. Buck Dawson: *The Complete Book of Dry-land Exercises for Swimming* (PELHAM BOOKS).
2. J. M. Hogg: *Land Conditioning for Competitive Swimming* (EP PUBLISHING LTD.).

13
Turns and stroke transitions

Whereas a competitor in a single-stroke event has only one type of turn to think about and to execute in his race, the individual medley swimmer has several. For there are three different turns in the 200 metres individual medley (L.C.) and seven in the 400 metres (L.C.).

These are:

200 metres (L.C.)

1. butterfly to backstroke
2. backstroke to breaststroke
3. breaststroke to freestyle

400 metres (L.C.)

1. butterfly to butterfly
2. butterfly to backstroke
3. backstroke to backstroke
4. backstroke to breaststroke
5. breaststroke to breaststroke
6. breaststroke to freestyle
7. freestyle to freestyle

All turns should be executed as near perfect as possible at all times during training. And it is necessary to be very specific, which means doing practices consisting of just turn work, so that total effort and concentration can be given to this part of the individual medley. The three turns involving turning from one stroke to another stroke need particular attention.

Individual medley events in competition are often won on the ability to turn well, particularly in short-course events.

1. Individual medley start as for butterfly

Fig. 23.

(i) Take up a position at the back of the block.
(ii) On the command 'Take your marks', step forward, gripping the front of the starting block with the toes. The feet are hip-width apart and the trunk bent forward at the waist with a slight bend of the knees. The arms are straight and hanging loosely, the palms of the hands facing backwards. The eyes focus 10–15 yards down the pool.
(iii) At the sound of the starter's gun or buzzer, the arms start their wind-up, moving through an upwards, outwards and swinging forwards motion. At this point the eyes look directly down at the feet. As the heels rise the centre of gravity starts to move forward.

Fig. 24.

Fig. 25.

(iv) As the arms pass the knees in their forward swing, the knees start to 'unwind' from their crouch position as the body moves into full extension. There should be a feeling of driving the feet into the starting block.

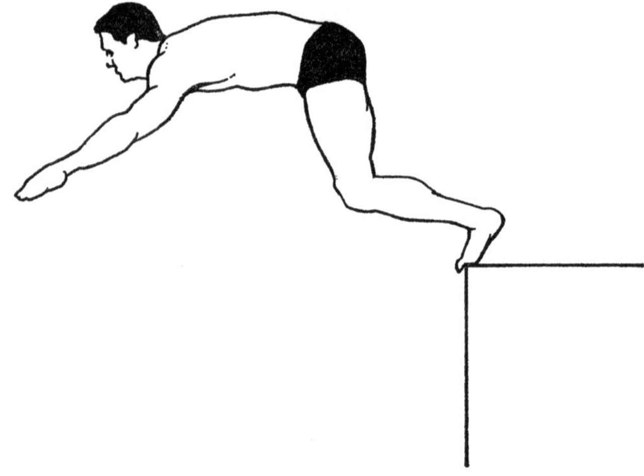

Fig. 26.

(v) As the ankles extend the body takes a flight position. The normal flight-path is slightly upwards.

Fig. 27.

(vi) Once the body is in flight and completely extended, the head is snapped down between the arms and it continues on its downward flight.

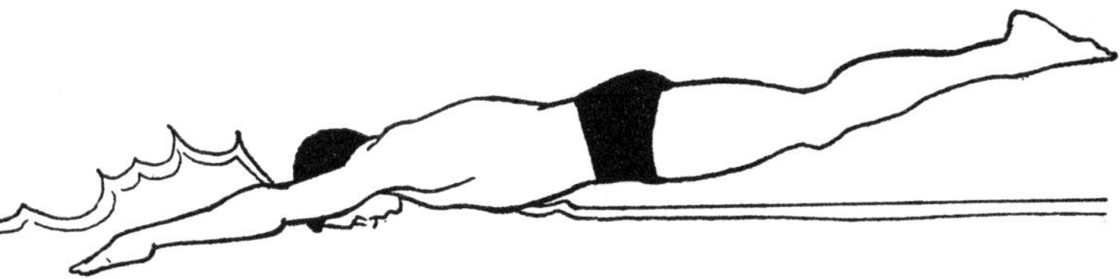

(vii) Entry is made with the fingers, followed by the arms, head, shoulders and body, making a 'clean' entry.

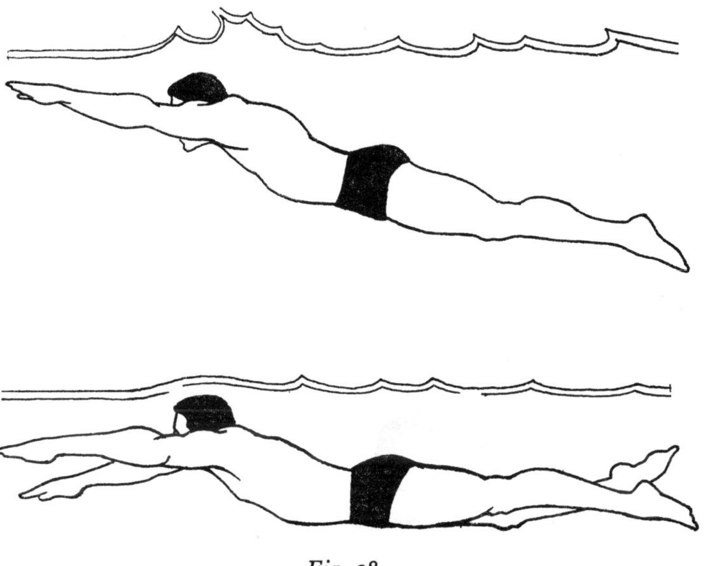

Fig. 28.

2. Butterfly to butterfly

(i) As the swimmer comes into the wall the hands must touch simultaneously and on the same level. The head is pushed

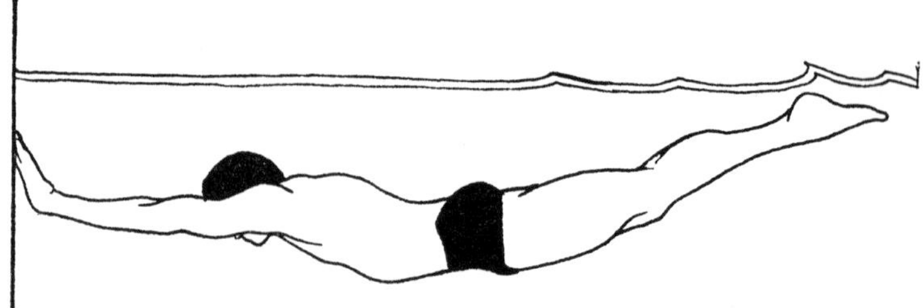

Fig. 29.

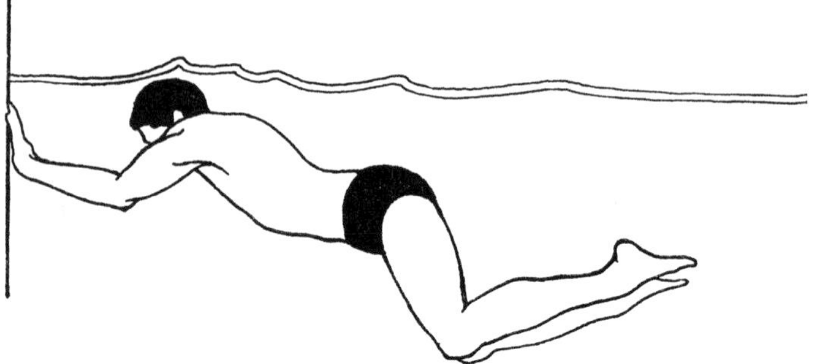

Fig. 30.

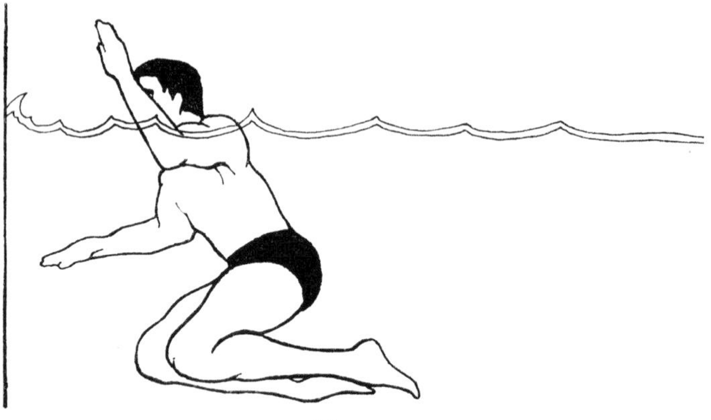

Fig. 31.

down between the arms momentarily and the knees begin to tuck and start to draw forward. The arm on the turning side is pulled backwards, the body turning onto its side.

126

Fig. 32.

(ii) As the body lies at 90° to the surface of the water, the legs are swung in towards the wall. The hand on the wall gives a slight push, moving the shoulders away from the wall. This arm swings over the water on recovery.

Fig. 33.

(iii) The feet are planted on the wall just as the arm-recovery is completed. At this point the body is completely swung around with the shoulders horizontal to the surface of the water. The arms are completely extended, head down, chin tucked in.

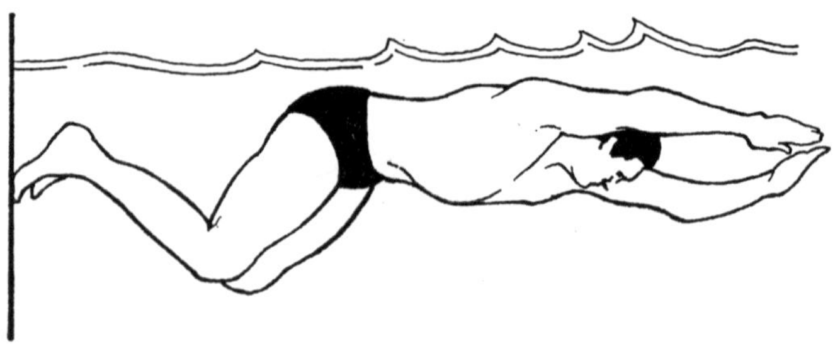

Fig. 34.

(iv) Straightening of the knees initiates the driving away from the wall.

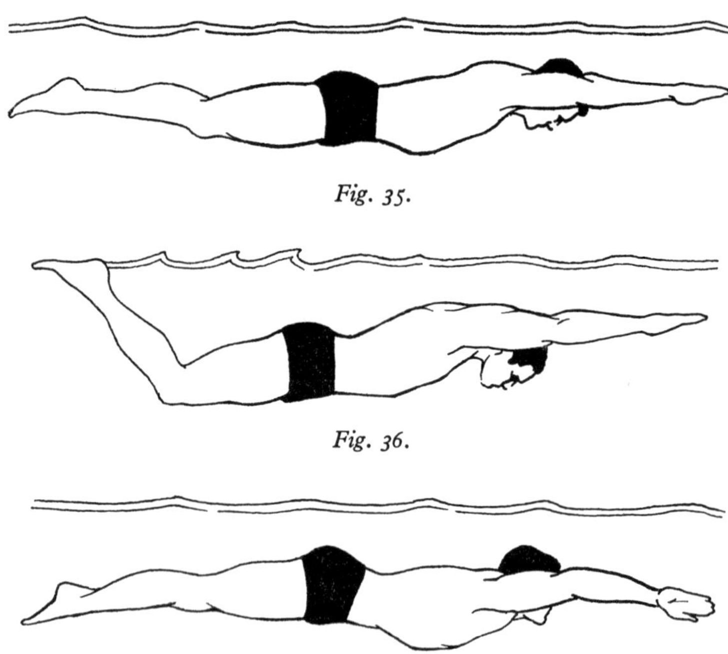

Fig. 35.

Fig. 36.

Fig. 37.

3. Butterfly to backstroke

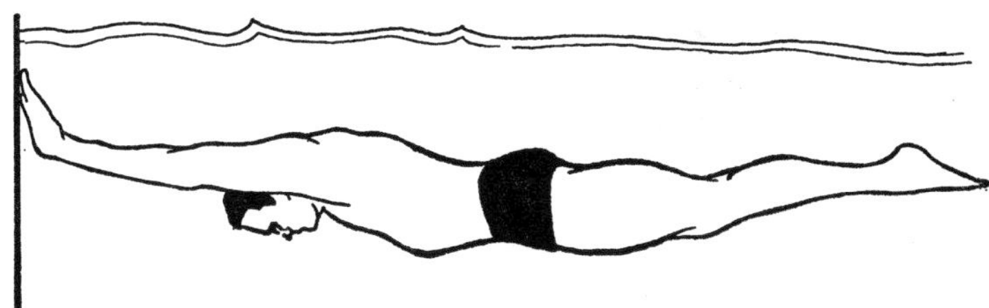

Fig. 38.

(i) Approach the wall in the same way as for the legal two-handed butterfly touch.

Fig. 39.

(ii) On contact with the wall, press the head down into the water slightly, pulling the chin down towards the chest. At this point the knees are drawn forward into a tucked position underneath the chest.

(iii) As the knees move forward the arms are beginning to push away from the wall, the head starting to 'unroll' with a

Fig. 40.

full extension of the neck. The body is kept relatively low to the surface of the water.

Fig. 41.

(iv) As the arms extend the feet come into contact with the wall. The hands leave the wall in a slight push-back, recovery of the arms being made just above the surface. The hands leave the wall just prior to the feet coming in contact.

An interesting scene at the World Aquatic Championships, 1973. Here coach Snelling and Leslie discuss race tactics during warm-up. Stephen Holland of Australia, 15 year-old world record holder of 800 and 1500 metres freestyle with coach Laurie Lawrence stand immediately behind. British coach David Haller and Brian Brinkley—Britain's most versatile male swimmer 1972/3 are seen standing in the middle of the photo, with Australian coach Forbes Carlile second from the right of the photo.

Swimming close to the lane-marker can sometimes act as motivation in a tough race. It brings a swimmer closer to the competitor in the next lane.

Leslie Cliff being tested for degree of back flexion by Dr. Eric Banister (left) Kinesiology Dept. Head, Simon Fraser University, Vancouver.

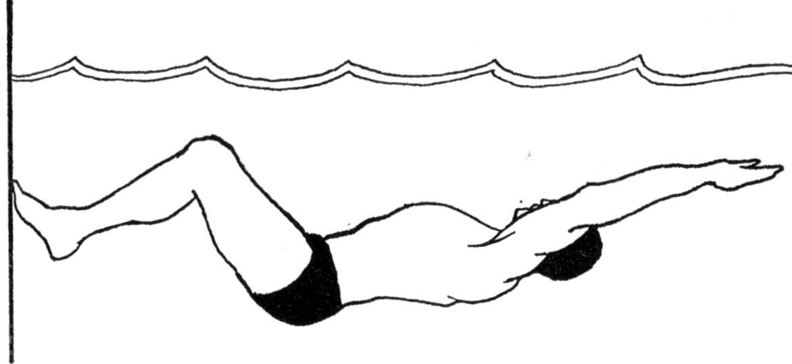

Fig. 42.

(v) At this point the legs start to drive as the knees start to straighten. Push the feet into the wall to generate as much power and speed as possible. The arms synchronize with the push-off, going back into the overhead position. This creates a streamlined position for the backstroke glide.

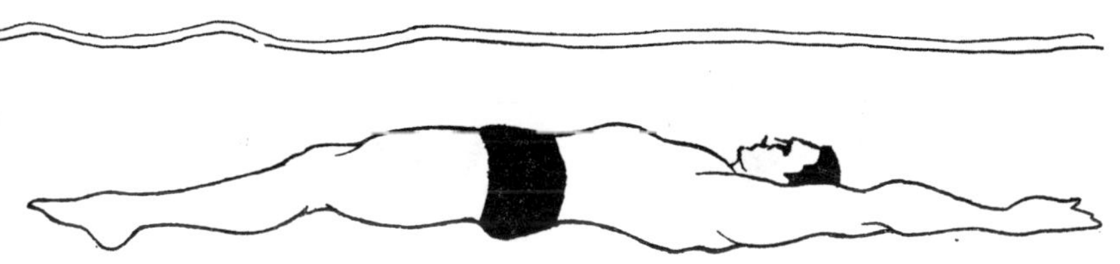

Fig. 43.

Common fault: trying to lift the body high out of the water on the 'fly touch'. With the body in a lower position there is more support from the up-thrust of the water.

4. *Backstroke to backstroke*

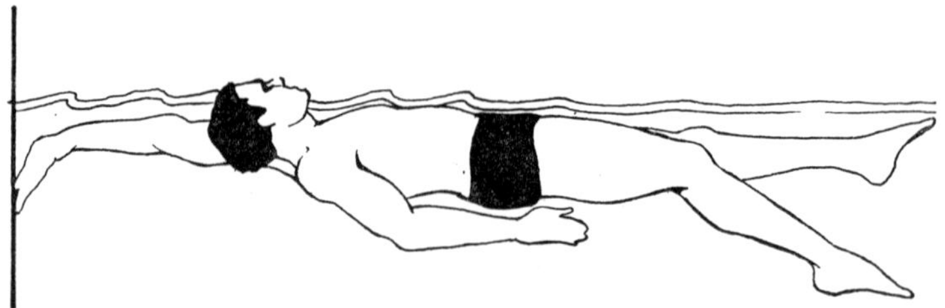

Fig. 44.

(i) Approach the wall maintaining momentum. Place one hand flat against the wall, close to the surface, fingers pointed inwards. As contact is made there is a slight 'give' at the elbow. The head is moved backwards, allowing the eyes to see the point of hand-contact.

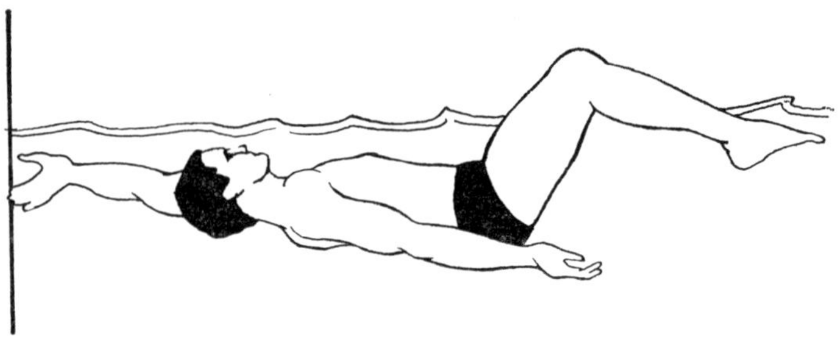

Fig. 45.

(ii) The knees are drawn up out of the water and as the feet break the surface pivotting of the body takes place allowing the legs to be swung over the surface of the water and in towards the wall.

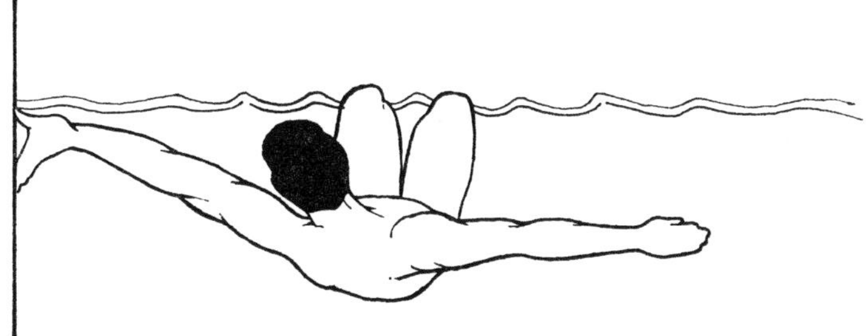

Fig. 46.

(iii) The hand is withdrawn from the wall just prior to the feet making contact. The feet are placed on the wall on the spot where the hands were.

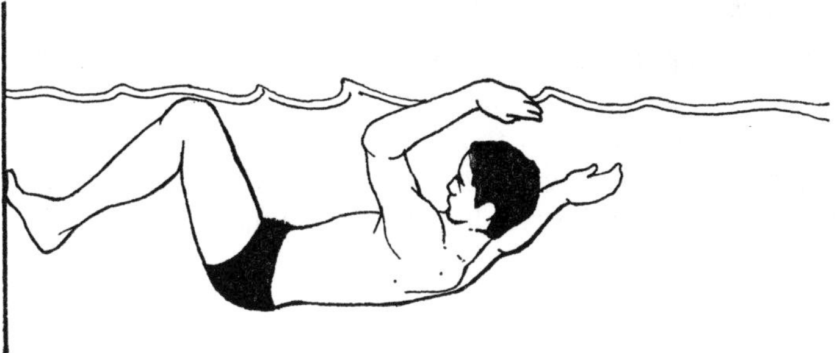

Fig. 47.

(iv) The arm and hand that remained at the side of the body are used to 'scoop' the water strongly. The hand appears to be forced towards the head. This assists in speeding up the turn.

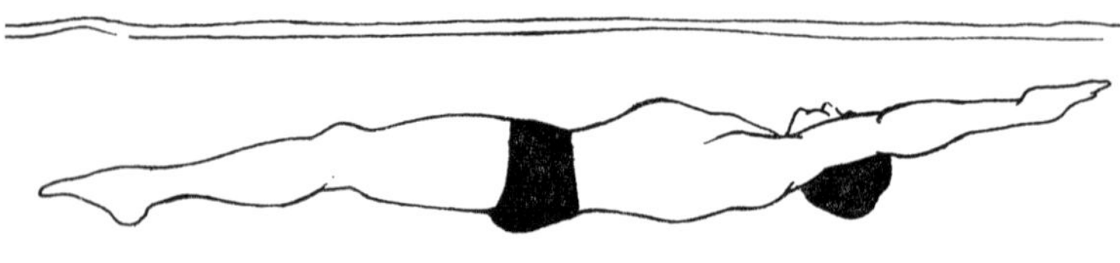

Fig. 48.

(v) A strong push-off from the wall now takes place, with the whole body in a fully extended, streamlined position.

5. *Backstroke to breaststroke*

(i) As the approach is made on backstroke and the lead hand makes contact with the wall, the fingers are pushed approximately 12 inches below the surface. The body is completely extended, with the head and shoulders sinking slightly below the surface, with the eyes looking approximately at the point of hand-contact.

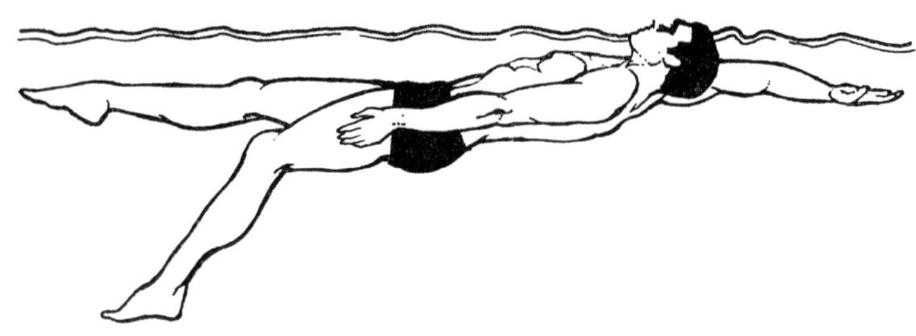

Fig. 49.

(ii) The knees together are drawn out of the water and pulled in towards the wall following the normal line of the body. The legs stay together throughout this movement.

Fig. 50.

(iii) As the feet clear the water, the body pivots—a half-twist, half-somersault takes place. The hand leaves the wall as the feet come directly over the top of the head. The free arm (the one not used in the hand-touch) remains stationary throughout the execution of the turn.

Fig. 51.

(iv) As the feet come down towards the wall, the arms are brought together in an extended position. As the feet come into contact with the wall the knees, which were held at an angle of slightly less than 90°, start to extend. There should be a strong push-off.

Fig. 52.

(v) The body pushes away from the wall in an extended position and the underwater breaststroke stroke is now executed as explained in the breaststroke turn.

Technical point: The body position must be in accordance with the rules for breaststroke—as described in breaststroke turn.

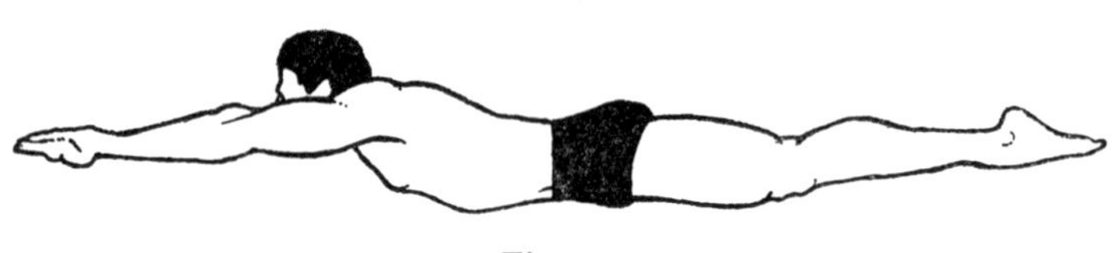

Fig. 53.

Important point: A good lungful of air should be taken prior to submersion of the head, as this is a long period underwater.

6. Breaststroke to breaststroke

N.B.: the breaststroke turn is executed in the same way as the butterfly turn, but on leaving the wall on the push-off the body glides downwards slightly to a depth sufficient to allow for the effective long underwater stroke.

(i) As the body extends completely underwater the palms turn outwards. The arms are pressed outwards to just wide of shoulder-width.
(ii) From this position the arms bend at the elbows and the hands are brought inwards. The upper arm remains stationary, the hands and forearms scooping around and inwards.
(iii) At this point the arms are brought to just below the chest.
(iv) From here the hands and forearms drive the water directly backwards towards the feet. The hands turn inwards and upwards, finishing by the thighs. From this point the hands and arms stay in close to the body.
(v) The recovery is made by sliding the hands close into the body (for streamlining) and as the hands pass the head in their forward recovery movement, the knees are bent and the heels are brought up into a cocked position.
(vi) The final extension of the arms and the drive of the leg-kick is simultaneously timed. This completes the allowed one full stroke underwater. Observe Fig. 30 (Butterfly to butterfly). The turn is the same up to Fig. 35.

7. Breaststroke to freestyle
(i) Approach the wall with the hands touching at the same time and on the same level. Pivoting immediately starts as the hands touch, the body remaining fairly low in the water.
(ii) The hand on the turning side makes only a light touch to the wall, this hand being immediately withdrawn following contact.
(iii) The elbow is pulled backwards and in towards the body. At the same time the head is drawn backwards, the chin turning in and tucking towards the shoulder. This initiates a pivoting of the body so that during the drive away from the wall it is 90° to the surface of the water—similar to the open freestyle turn. On leaving the wall the other arm is brought up over the surface in recovery to join the other arm for the push-off and extension.
(iv) Two arm-pulls are made before the head turns to inhale again—this to avoid the turbulence.

8. *Freestyle to freestyle*

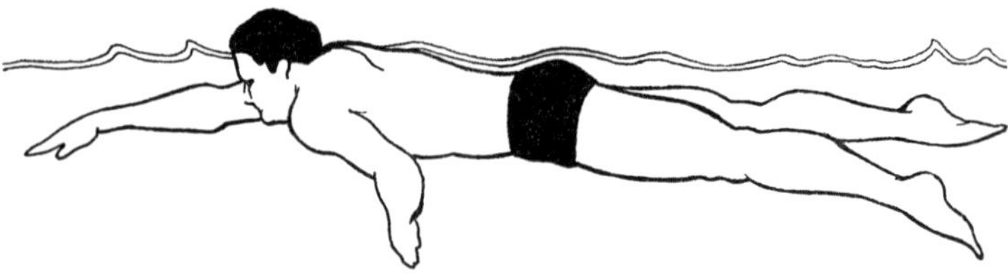

Fig. 54.

(i) At the point the decision to turn is made one hand stays by the side of the body, not making its recovery.

Fig. 55.

(ii) The forward arm is then also brought down to the side of the body.

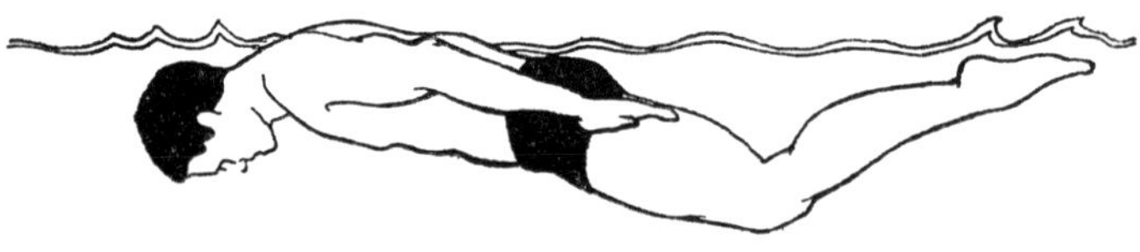

Fig. 56.

(iii) At this point the head is vigorously snapped downwards, completely stopping forward momentum, the eyes looking backwards underneath the water. The body remains shallow to the surface.

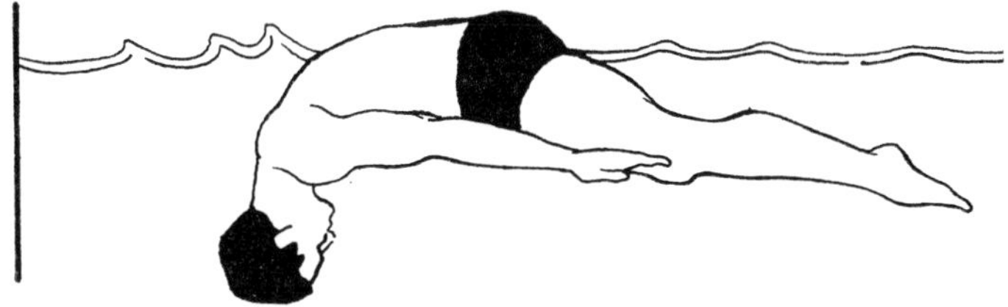

Fig. 57.

(iv) The hips are piked and as the head come under the seat, a ¼-twist of the body is made.

Fig 58.

(v) The legs are drawn up over the surface of the water in a tucked position. At this point as the legs travel towards the wall the twisting of the body is assisted by scooping water with the hand nearest the surface.

Fig. 59.

139

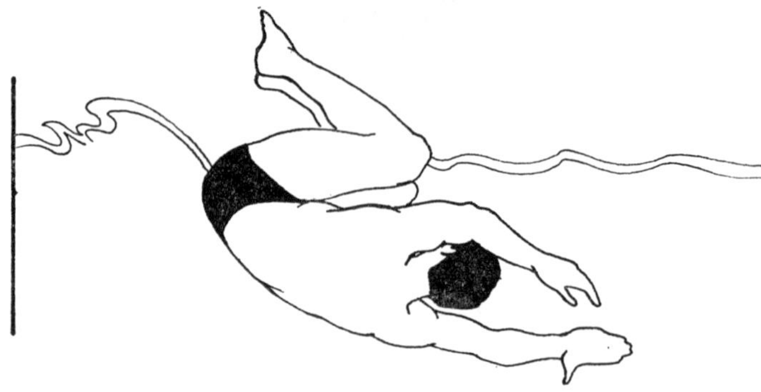

Fig. 60.

(vi) As the feet travel towards the wall, the legs start their extension and a kicking action takes place. This driving of the legs on impact eliminates any pause and speeds up the turn.

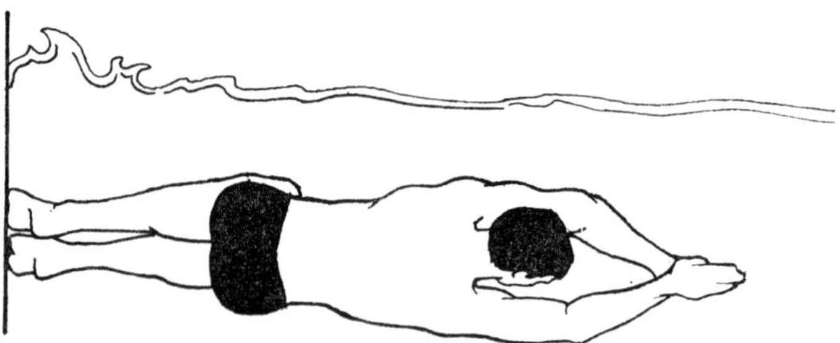

Fig. 61.

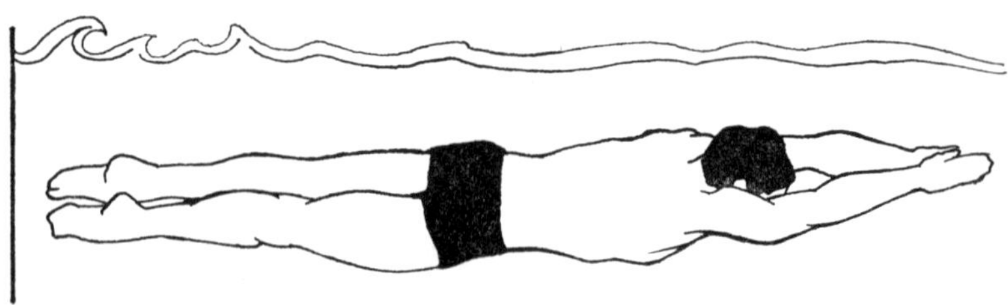

Fig. 62.

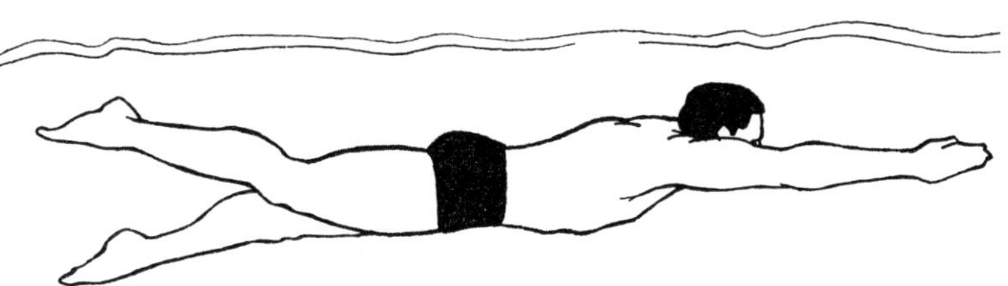

Fig. 63.

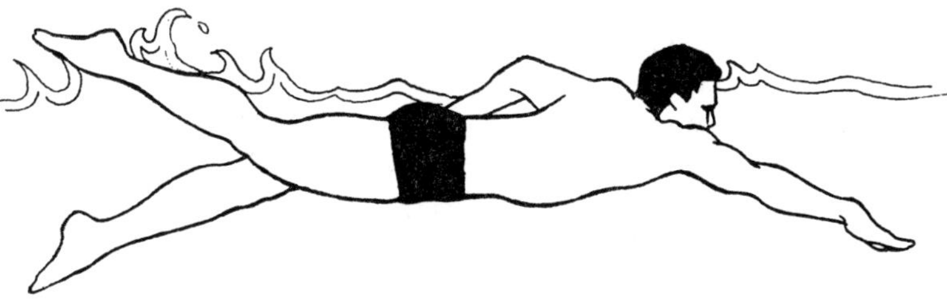

Fig. 64.

(vii) Push-off is made at an angle of 90° to the surface (Fig. 61) and as extension of the body takes place during the glide phase, it rotates back to the normal frontcrawl position (Figs 62–64).

14

Personal theories and reflections on Individual Medley

In pre-planning for race tactics or meet strategy for individual medley events, there are three main things to know and work on:

1. You must know your own strengths and weaknesses in order to understand what you could be capable of doing in relation to tactics.

2. Really try and understand as much as possible about the opposition you are planning to use your tactics against. Try and find out the type of splits they have used in previous races and if there is any regular pattern to previous swims. This can be very helpful. Any up-to-date information on how well they have been training will give you some indication of where their strengths and weaknesses are likely to be. For instance, if you know they have been working fairly hard right up to the last minute of competition, you know they probably haven't had the opportunity to do the sprint work. This type of thing helps you to possibly take an early advantage in the race.

3. No matter what plan you might come up with, you must be practising in the early competitions and in practice workouts the variable paces you might have to use for a tactical race. Also, you must be flexible and have an alternative plan in case the tactics you had planned are not effective for some reason. Have enough flexibility to be able to change your plan if necessary. If possible it is good to be able to control the race and this is something that will only come with experience. On some occasions you can slow down a race to such a point that you can take the 'sting' out of your opponents' best strokes. But to be able to employ this type of tactic you have to be able to rely on having a faster sprint than anyone else in the later stages of the race, otherwise you can find that your own strategy can 'backfire' on you.

400 metres individual medley
If you are not going to try and use any tactic to upset or disturb the confidence of the people you are racing against, I have found that a tactic to use in order to get a good performance in the 400 I.M. is built around the idea of taking the butterfly out relatively easily. It seems to be important that a swimmer should be feeling good at the end of the butterfly leg in order to have the ability to put the next three strokes together to achieve a good overall result. It is good to still be out with the field at the end of the 'fly, so practising taking the butterfly out as fast as possible at the beginning of the season—particularly in the less-important meets—is a good way of preparing for this type of swim.

200 metres individual medley
The above is not quite the tactic we would use in the 200 I.M. I have found that in this event the best way is to swim flat out right from the start. There is not enough time to take any stroke out easily, you have to be 'wound up' ready to go right at the beginning of the 'fly. I find that using this kind of tactic the freestyle leg isn't finished as fast as could be hoped for. However, taking everything into account, it does seem to be the best way to swim the race.

In the 400 metres individual medley, assuming the butterfly leg has been taken out reasonably easily from the point of turning onto the backstroke, we use a build-up concept—realizing that the second 50 of each 100 is going to be as fast or faster than the first 50. This is a transition problem and also it is a controlled situation, where we are trying to be more even-paced. And in the individual medley we have to look at the splitting of the 100 on each individual stroke as being a negative split type of swim. And each stroke should be swum with more effort than the one before. This is a continuous build-up in applied effort throughout the whole swim and one of the best ways to swim the 400 I.M.

In some races you can find yourself see-sawing out in front, falling behind, back in front again and so on—on each stroke.

But regardless of where you are in the field, the build-up of pace principle should be followed. Swim with as much control as possible to the end of the 300 metres. Mentally we are usually looking at this as a 300 race, relying on fitness, training and endurance work to 'bring us home' on the last 100 freestyle. I find this seems to produce the best times.

One way to use tactics against the opposition is to work in the following way. Take the race out fast in the beginning. By doing this you are putting some sort of psychological strain on the opposition, making them wonder if they should go out with you. And just by placing them in this position you have them a little unsettled. If you take the race out at a fast pace, the opposition will have to decide whether you will 'drop dead', and allow you to build up a big lead or accept your challenge and go with you. This can un-nerve them and destroy any pre-plan they may have had.

If you have made this fast start to your race and you want to hold the momentum, you have to 'feel' the opposition who may have been caught 'off guard' in making their effort to close the gap. And usually at the point where you have made a break it is a good idea to allow the opposition to draw close again and you should realize that to do so they have probably been forced into an unexpected rhythm. And if it is possible a second move at this point can be a decisive one. Once they have drawn level you probably 'have' the race if you can pick up the pace again. Of course, this is very tough on you. Particularly if your opposition is responding well to this type of tactic—you yourself have to live with the pace and effort that you applied at the beginning of the race. But it is a very effective tactic and can really disturb a swimmer who is mentally less-tough.

General tactics
A fast/slow tactic is sometimes possible, particularly if you are racing along-side the main competition. Unfortunately, in the I.M. in a large 50 metre pool, it is possible to be at one end of the pool with the main opposition in the far end lane up to

20–25 metres away. And under these conditions it can be difficult to judge where you are in relation to the opposition. Except as a rule, if you are way out ahead in the backstroke you are able to tip your head a little to take at least a slight 'peep' down the field to get some indication as to where you are without spoiling the stroke. Or in the breaststroke you can take a slight look. But you must be careful. For one thing, while you are thinking out these things you are not able to give full concentration to your stroke technique and this might suffer because of your divided attention. You will have to decide for yourself whether looking is justifiable.

When you hit the freestyle leg it is a good idea to breathe on alternate sides. It has the advantage that you don't have a 'blind' side, and you can't be caught up quickly by someone you were not aware of. But if you are in any sort of oxygen debt, taking a breath every third stroke is not advisable.

If you are fairly evenly matched with the opposition, a good time to try to make a break is immediately following a turn. In the underwater part of the drive, a really good push-off and 'cutting' the underwater stroke can sometimes just give you that extra two or three feet in a race. It is possible, for-example, for a poor breaststroker with good turns and long push-offs from the wall, to excel in the 200 yards (short course) individual medley. Although he may be unable to do well in the 200 metres. But nobody can make it world-class today with a weak stroke of any kind in the 400 metres I.M. You pay a little for the extra effort you put into your turns, but if you can catch your opposition at a slow point you can sometimes gain enough distance to give you confidence. If you are in a winning position at this point it gives you a good 'winning attitude' and you are able to take real advantage of that slight move for the rest of the race.

One of the recent steps in progress in our sport is the electronic timing devices used at many major meets. The large scoreboards show splits, etc. and swimmers can take advantage of this. By watching the scoreboard during a race a swimmer can be 'pace coached'. It is easy during the I.M.—

on the breaststroke and backstroke legs—for an alert swimmer with keen eyesight to spot his running splits and understand exactly how he is going. This can be an advantage. If a swimmer is not swimming well, however, it could work as a disadvantage. But in most cases it works. This is not something to be actually recommended, but something that should be recognized as a possibility.

Try not to build up an oxygen debt at any time during the I.M., for the 400 particularly is a gruelling event. The final tactic at the end of a race is to swim the last strokes without lifting the head. In this way you can finish extremely fast in order to get every fraction of an inch out of your performance. In a closely-contested race, where thousandths of a second count, this is vital. The days of flaying the water fast and furiously at the finish of a race to speed up the reflexes and reactions of the manual time-keepers are over!

One thing that can help to give a swimmer a good feeling during a race is for him to ride close to the competitor in the next lane by swimming close to the lane-marker. And if you are close to the lane of a swimmer who is just ahead of you, you give the impression of being closer than you really are. Whereas if both swimmers are on opposite sides of 7 ft. wide lanes this can put them 13–14 ft. apart. So it can be a good idea to ride close to the lane of the next swimmer. It helps to give you the incentive to close the gap if you are behind in your race.

Pace plan and time comparisons for individual medley
This is the most difficult event for which to set up a pace plan chart. But a swimmer must try to understand his own pace potential, based on his stroke strengths and weaknesses in order to consider some kind of plan.

This is one way that I went about it for Leslie Cliff. I took 1972 as a base on which to work, as this was the year that she reached a world-class level of performance. And at this point I realized that we should have a new understanding of how to improve her times.

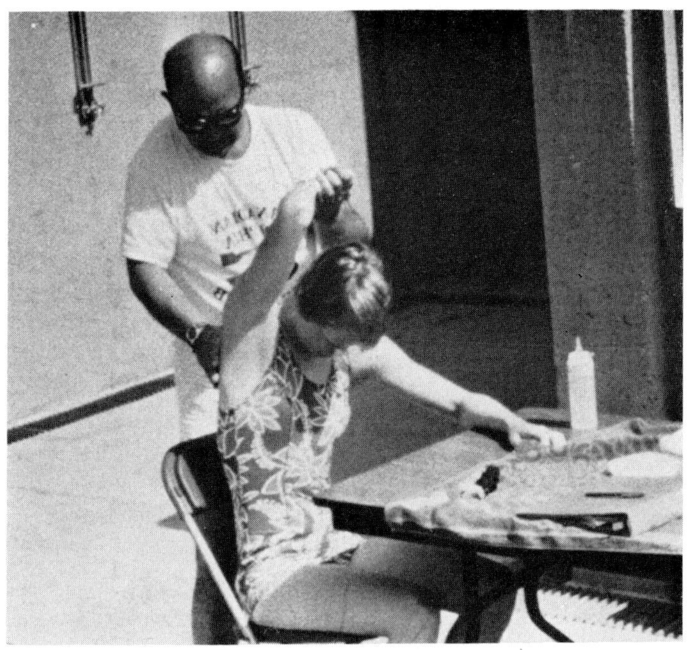

The masseur can be a great help during the taper period. When a swimmer feels 'loose' and relaxed he is in a more receptive frame of mind. Here Haik Gharibians, team physiotherapist and physiotherapist to Canadian National Teams, is seen massaging a swimmer.

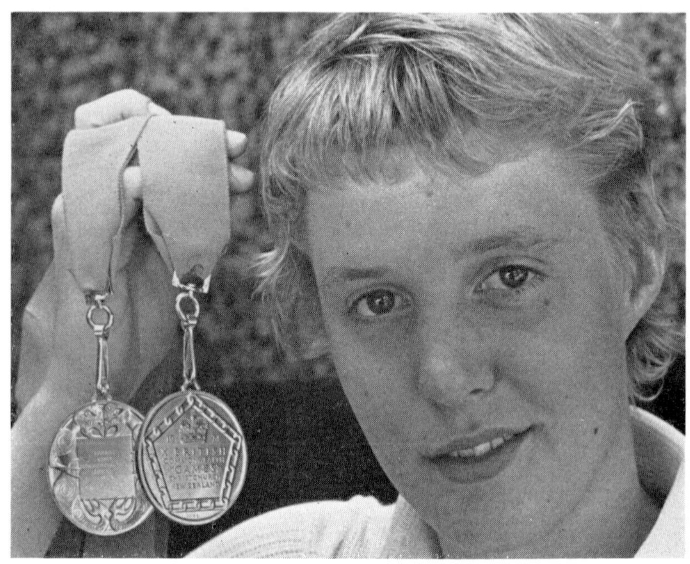

Above. *Leslie Cliff added to her gold medal successes at the Tenth Commonwealth Games held in Christchurch, New Zealand. She won the 200 and 400 metres Individual Medley events. In doing so she set a new Canadian and Commonwealth Games records in both events. She also turned in lifetime-best performances, clocking 2:24.13 for the 200 metres and 5:01.35 in the 400 metres. Here Leslie proudly displays her gold medals*

Left. *Wendy Cook is the latest star to come out of Deryk Snelling's programme. At the age of 17 she won three gold medals for Canada at the 1974 Commonwealth Games, setting a new world record for the 100 metres backstroke (1:04.78). She won a bronze medal in the same event at the first World Aquatic Championships in 1973 and is now looking towards Montreal*

*The following is the plan we came up with for the 400
metres I.M:*

Best 100 m. times (swum in competition)		Olympic Splits	Difference from best time	New proposed times for 100 m. races
100 m. 'fly	1:05.9	1:10.2	4.3	1:04.9
100 m. back	1:10.0	1:17.7	7.7	1:09.0
100 m. br.	1:20.6	1:28.7	8.1	1:19.6
100 m. free	1:01.7	1:06.8	5.1	1:00.7

Now as Leslie likes to swim all strokes in swim meets
during the season, we drew up what we would like to see her
swim 100 metre events down to in the next year. This would
take her time down to under five minutes. Taking one second
'across the board', it would read as above.

This is only one possibility. There are other ways, but in
all cases the likes and dislikes of the individual must be
considered when setting goals.

The above plan can be worked using 200 metres and
allowing for a three-second 'across the board' improvement.

I tried for a while to find a common denominator among the
champion individual medley swimmers, but as yet none
appears to exist. I feel that this is due largely to the fact that
this is a relatively new event and possibly due to a lack of
available statistics from which to draw new ideas.

One idea that I had was to look at the previous best performances of the swimmers who came first and second in the
individual medley events at the World Aquatic Championships. And I found that distance freestyle was the closest
event as far as a common denominator is concerned. I have
included a chart (page 148) showing this information for
your interest.

The charts on pages 149 and 150 give a comparison of
individual medley (400 metres) strokes *v.* individual strokes.

Chart Showing:

(a) 1st and 2nd place winners at the World Aquatic Games, 1973
(b) Their previous best performances

Name	Position at World Ch'ships	Event	100 Breast-stroke	200 Breast-stroke	100 Butter-fly	200 Butter-fly	100 Back-stroke	200 Back-stroke	200 I.M.	400 I.M.	100 f/s	200 f/s	400 f/s	800 / 1,500 f/s
G. Larsson age 22	1st	200 m. I.M. (men)						1970 2:13.3	1972 2:7.2	1972 4:32.0		1970 1:55.7	1970 4:2.6	1970 16:41.5
S. Carper age 20	2nd	200 m. I.M. (men)							1972 2:10.6					
A. Hargitay age 17	1st	400 m. I.M. (men)		1972 2:31.1	1972 58.5	1972 2:4.7			1972 2:9.7	1972 4:32.7		1971 1:58.8	1971 4:11.9	1972 16:44.6
R. Strachan age 18	2nd	400 m. I.M. (men)								1972 4:43.5			1972 4:08.6	1972 16:18.5
A. Huebner age 16	1st	200 m. I.M. (women)	1971 1:17.4						1972 2:31.2					
K. Ender age 15	2nd	200 m. I.M. (women)							1972 2:23.6	1972 5:16.2				1972 9:38.3
G. Wegner age 18	1st	400 m. I.M. (women)										1972 2:09.5	1972 4:23.1	1972 8:58.9
A. Franke age 16	2nd	400 m. I.M. (women)							1972 2:30.6	1972 5:13.4				1972 9:37.9

Women	Fly	Back	Breast	Free	Total	I.M.	Diff.	Comments
1952				1:04.6				
1953								
1954	1:16.6	long course swimming not in force						
1955		insufficient data available						
1956		1:12.9		1:02.0				
1957	1:10.5							
1958	1:09.6	1:11.9	1:19.6	1:01.2	4:42.3	5:43.7	61.4	Sylvia Ruuska
1959	1:09.1	1:11.4	1:19.6	1:01.2	4:41.3	5:40.2	58.9	
1960	1:09.1	1:09.0	1:19.0	1:00.2	4:37.3	5:36.5	59.2	Donna De Varona
1961	1:08.2	1:09.0	1:18.2	1:00.2	4:35.6	5:34.5	58.9	
1962	1:07.3	1:09.0	1:18.2	59.5	4:34.0	5:21.9	47.9	Donna De Varona
1963	1:06.1	1:08.9	1:18.2	59.5	4:31.5	5:21.9	50.4	
1964	1:04.7	1:07.7	1:17.2	58.9	4:28.5	5:14.9	46.4	
1965	1:04.5	1:07.7	1:16.5	58.9	4:27.6	5:14.9	47.3	
1966	1:04.5	1:07.4	1:15.6	58.9	4:26.4	5:14.9	48.5	
1967	1:04.5	1:07.1	1:14.6	58.9	4:25.1	5:08.2	43.1	Claudia Kolb
1968	1:04.5	1:06.2	1:14.2	58.9	4:23.8	5:04.7	40.9	Kolb was most advanced to date
1969	1:04.5	1:05.6	1:14.2	58.9	4:23.2	5:04.7	41.5	in relation to ind. strokes (up un-
1970	1:04.1	1:05.6	1:14.2	58.9	4:22.8	5:04.7	41.9	til the World Aquatic Champion-
1971	1:04.1	1:05.6	1:14.2	58.9	4:22.8	5:04.7	41.9	ships, September 1973)
1972	1:03.3	1:05.6	1:13.6	58.5	4:21.0	5:02.9	41.9	Gail Neall
1973	1:03.0	1:05.6	1:13.6	58.5	4:20.7	5:02.9	42.2	
1973	1:02.3	1:05.0	1:13.6	57.5	4:18.4	4:57.5	37.0	Gudrun Wegner

Comparison of Individual Medley vs. Strokes

Men	Fly	Back	Breast	Free	Total	I.M.	Diff.	Comments
1952		1:03.3		55.4				
1953	1:04.3	1:03.3	1:10.9	55.4	4:13.9	5:32.1	78.2	
1954	1:02.3	1:02.8	1:09.8	54.8	4:09.7	5:32.1		
1955	1:01.5	1:02.8	1:08.2	54.8	4:07.3			
1956	1:01.5	1:02.2	1:08.2	55.4	4:06.7			
1957	1:01.2	1:02.2	1:11.5	54.6	4:09.5	5:12.9	63.4	
1958	1:00.1	1:01.5	1:11.5	54.6	4:07.7	5:12.9	65.2	
1959	1:00.1	1:01.5	1:11.5	54.6	4:07.7	5:08.8	61.1	Ian Black
1960	58.7	1:01.5	1:11.5	54.6	4:06.3	5:04.5	58.2	
1961	58.6	1:01.3	1:07.5	53.6	4:01.0	4:55.6	54.6	Ted Stickles
1962	57.0	1:00.9	1:07.5	53.6	3:59.0	4:51.0	52.0	
1963	57.0	1:00.9	1:07.5	53.6	3:59.0	4:50.2	51.2	
1964	57.0	59.6	1:06.9	52.9	3:56.4	4:45.4	49.0	Dick Roth
1965	57.0	59.6	1:06.9	52.9	3:56.4	4:45.4	49.0	
1966	57.0	59.6	1:06.9	52.9	3:56.4	4:45.4	49.0	
1967	55.7	58.4	1:06.7	52.6	3:53.4	4:45.4	52.0	
1968	55.6	58.0	1:06.4	52.2	3:52.2	4:39.0	46.8	Charlie Hickcox
1969	55.6	57.8	1:05.8	52.2	3:51.4	4:33.9	42.5	Gary Hall
1970	55.6	56.9	1:05.8	51.9	3:50.2	4:31.0	40.8	Hall most advanced in relation
1971	55.0	56.7	1:05.8	51.9	3:49.4	4:31.0	41.6	to ind. strokes
1972	54.3	56.3	1:04.9	51.2	3:46.7	4:30.8	44.1	Current record should drop to

15

(i) Ideal splits for the Individual Medley

(researched by Steven C. Saur)

(ii) Pace Plan for a 200 yd. Individual Medley

(researched by John P. Hussey)

Ideal Splits for the Individual Medley

In his book, *The Science of Swimming*, James Counsilman presents an 'Even Pace Chart' for splits in races of various distances, advocating an 'even pace' as the most economical application of energy to the entire distance of the race. As a coach, I have found this to be a valuable concept: my experience would bear it out as far superior to the 'bust-out-and-die' method of swimming a race. Moreover in view of a majority of recent record-setting swims, I wonder if Doctor Counsilman might be tempted to revise his chart even more toward the 'negative split' or 'balanced-split' as the ideal.

In the same book, Doc Counsilman, in discussing the Individual Medley, describes it as the most 'interesting of events'. He shows a few I.M. splits, but explicitly avoids indicating any ideal race patterns, because of the differing stroke strengths of each individual swimmer. I submit that such a theoretical pacing chart *can* be drawn up, and can be of some value to coach and swimmer.

Even-strength, Even-pace Splits
If we accept Doc Counsilman's formula for an even-paced 200 yard swim of a certain stroke (i.e. 1st Quadrant + 2 second

151

= 2nd Quadrant; 1st Quadrant + 3 seconds = 3rd and 4th Quadrants), there is a not-too-complicated method by which we can construct a set of ideal splits for the 200 yard I.M. race.

STEP ONE: Take the present American Records for the 200 yard swim of each of the four strokes. (Round off to whole seconds for simplicity):

Butterfly	1:48.0	Breaststroke	2:04.0
Backstroke	1:50.0	Freestyle	1:38.0

STEP TWO: Using Counsilman's formula (given above), construct 'even-pace' splits for each of these times:

Butterfly	25.0	27.0	28.0	28.0
Backstroke	25.5	27.5	28.5	28.5
Breaststroke	29.0	31.0	32.0	32.0
Freestyle	22.5	24.5	25.5	25.5

STEP THREE: From these splits, take the proper Quadrant time for each stroke:

Butterfly	(1st Quadrant)	25.0	
Backstroke	(2nd Quadrant)	27.5	
Breaststroke	(3rd Quadrant)	32.0	
Freestyle	(4th Quadrant)	25.5	Total time: 1:50.0

This means that by adding these 'ideal pace' Quadrants, we can arrive at a projected I.M. time for a swimmer who swims all four strokes at American Record levels. More importantly, we have established a ratio of each stroke's time to the other, based upon the existing records for each stroke. Maintaining the same time ratio of strokes, we can then construct a table of splits for a 'balanced' even-paced I.M. swim at different speed levels:

	Decimal % of Total								
Fly	227	25.0	26.1	27.2	28.4	29.5	30.6	31.8	32.9	34.0
Back	250	27.5	28.7	30.0	31.2	32.5	33.8	35.0	36.2	37.5
Breast	291	32.0	33.5	34.9	36.4	37.8	39.3	40.7	42.2	43.6
Free	232	25.5	26.7	29.0	30.2	31.3	32.5	33.7	34.9	34.9
Total	1,000	1:50.0	1:55.0	2:00.0	2:05.0	2:10.0	2:15.0	2:20.0	2:25.0	2:30.0

By interpolating this chart for the time done by any swimmer, or by merely using the decimal ratios, the coach can ascertain which strokes are swum faster or slower than a perfect-balanced race.

Individualized Even-pace Splits

The second way to utilize this mathematical concept is to construct 'even-pace' splits based on an individual swimmer's strokes, accepting some as stronger or weaker, comparatively, than some others. The same formula can be 'plugged in' as was done with the American Record times—take the swimmer's best 200 yard times for each stroke, derive 'even-pace' splits, and combine the respective Quadrant times to obtain the ratios for that swimmer's ideal I.M. splits.

However, there is one practical drawback to employing this method. This lies in the fact that most swimmers do not perform proportionately well at the 200 yard distance for all four strokes. Most swimmers will do rather poorly with their weaker strokes over the 200 yard distance, despite the ratio of stroke speed for shorter distances. I have therefore found it advantageous, especially for high school swimmers, to construct 'fictional' 200 yard times for each swimmer, based on his relative speed at shorter distances. These are mathematically derived as follows: Take the American Record for each stroke at the shorter (here 100 yards) distance and the longer (200 yard) distance, and derive a ratio of longer to horter times for each stroke. (Again, I have rounded off for simplicity.)

	100 yd. A.R.	*200 yd. A.R.*	*Long/Short Ratio*
Butterfly	49.0	1:48.0	2.204
Backstroke	51.0	1:50.0	2.157
Breaststroke	57.0	2:04.0	2.075
Freestyle	45.0	1:38.0	2.078

By applying these long/short ratios to the individual swimmer's 100 yard times for each stroke, we derive a 'fictional'

200 yard time which more truly reflects the relative stroke strengths of a swimmer who is more accustomed to the 100 yard distances for all strokes. We can then apply the rest of the formula for deriving even-pace splits as above.

To illustrate this, let us take an average swimmer whose 100 yard times are known, and work out an individualized I.M. split table for him.

Subject: *John Doe*, age 16.

	Actual *100 yard* *Times*		*Long/* *Short* *Ratios*		*'Fictional'* *200 yard* *Times*
Butterfly	58.6	×	2.204	=	2:09.2
Backstroke	59.0	×	2.157	=	2:07.3
Breaststroke	1:07.5	×	2.175	=	2:26.8
Freestyle	5.04	×	2.178	=	1:54.0

Now let's apply the 'even-pace' I.M. idea to John with his individual strengths and weaknesses:

	Q1	*Q2*	*Q3*	*Q4*	*Final Time*
Butterfly	30.25	32.25	33.25	33.25	2:09.0
Backstroke	29.75	31.75	32.75	32.75	2:07.0
Breaststroke	34.75	36.75	37.75	37.75	2:27.0
Freestyle	26.50	28.50	29.50	29.50	1:54.0

Ideal Splits: 30.25, 31.75, 37.75, 29.50 for a 2:09.3

This means that not only should John be able to do a 2:09.3 I.M. but also that at the present relative strengths of his strokes the above time-ratios between strokes seem ideal for even pace. We can then construct an improvement chart for John, based on the present ratios of his strokes to each other (*see* top of facing page).

Needless to say, both of these uses of this mathematical approach take no account of psychological factors such as opponent 'psyching', individual 'feel', and attitudes towards the strokes; these formulas treat the swimmer as a machine. But then it seems to me that the greatest progress in our sport today—especially as pertains to the records currently being set—occurs precisely where our swimmers have become the most machine-like in their approach to pace.

	Decimal Ratio to Total Time	John Doe's Actual	Pro-jected Ideal Splits	Projected Improved Times		
Fly	.234	27.8 actual *30.8 proj'd*	30.25	29.5	28.8	28.1
Back	.246	35.3 actual *32.4 proj'd*	31.75	31.0	30.3	29.5
Breast	.292	42.2 actual *38.4 proj'd*	37.75	36.8	35.9	35.0
Free	.228	26.3 actual *30.0 proj'd*	29.50	28.7	28.0	27.4
Total	1.000	*2:11.6*	2:09.30	2:06.0	2:03.0	2:00.0

Pace Plan for a 200 yard Individual Medley

Because of its varying skills and rates of speed, a pace chart has never been set up for that four stroke monster, the Individual Medley. And, such a chart could only be a guide, as the swimmer's ability in each stroke must be considered along with other factors. However, in a search to find an answer to the problem, a method was tried, and when put into effect, the results were most gratifying. Despite the results, it was realized that a single shot deal was not a valid premise, contention or result. It did, however, lead to a four-year study and more practical use. Both sustained the original thinking.

The first pace plan was set-up in the spring of 1963 in an attempt to have a swimmer realize his full potential in his championship meet. He was of the 'Go out and hang on school' and would go out in 27 seconds for his first fifty'fly. He would turn in a 2:21 or a 2:22 for the event. He was prevailed upon to go out in 28 plus and he dropped to 2:16 the first time he tried it. In the finals he dropped to 2:14. This change was in the matter of a week or two. Another youngster did

2:32 in the trials of a meet and qualified sixth. He was prevailed upon to use the pace plan in the finals and dropped to 2:24 as he moved up to third place despite the fact the 2.32 had been his fastest previous time. Other instances have shown equal results.

These are not considered great times, but they are the times that most High School coaches must contend with. And, since improvement is there, it must be considered. The main error made in the event is taking it out too fast. In working on this, it was not only found that the novices erred in this, but it was found that when our top-flight swimmers controlled the earlier part, their race, their final time was better. This can be noted if you compare Jastremski's in 1962 and 1963. Here is a stroke comparison:

| 1962 | 24.5/24.5 | 31.7/56.2 | 34.3/1:30.5 | 29.6/1:59.4 |
| 1963 | 25.2/25.2 | 32.0/57.2 | 33.4/1:30.6 | 27.9/1:58.5 |

Note how much faster he came back in the freestyle in '63. Of course, he could have been in better condition. The slower early pace cannot be ignored, however.

The study showed that the slower the final time, the faster the swimmer actually went out. The faster the final, the more controlled was the initial effort of the swimmer. On a percentage basis of their final time, the slower swimmers went out as much as 2 per cent faster than the top flight swimmers. Disregarding the physchological, physical, and other reasons for this, we must accept the tables below for what they are, and interpret them the best we know how. They certainly indicate that a swimmer must control his energy output in his first 50 if he is to turn in his best time.

The tables are made up of the times of all entries in the men's A.A.U. National Indoor Championships for the last four years and in the Michigan Class 'A' High School Championships for the last three years. These are the years that both groups used time standards for entry. This made a total of 124 swimmers for the Men's Nationals and 66 for the High School Championships, for a group total of 190 of our better swimmers in the study. The proficiency in the various strokes would vary with this number of swimmers. A larger sampling would be better, and the study will continue. But it was found that when the old entries in the pre-standard days were used, the figures were extremely unreliable, as some swimmers seemed to enter the event only to get a free ticket to the meet.

Below are tables comparing the entries in the National and the High School Championships. In Table I the average times for each stroke is listed, followed by the average split and final times for each category of swimmer. The field groups include every entry for a total of 66 H.S. and 124 A.A.U. swimmers. The finalists are the top six—followed by the last six and the winners.

Table I

Average stroke times and splits

Group	Field	Finalists	Last Six	Winners
Fly				
H.S.	26.1	26.9	28.3	25.9
A.A.U.	26.3	25.8	27.5	25.2
Back				
H.S.	34.5/62.6	33.6/60.5	35.6/63.2	30.9/56.8
A.A.U.	31.7/58.0	31.0/56.8	34.1/61.3	30.0/55.2
Breast				
H.S.	41.7/1:44.5	40.0/1:40.5	43.0/1:47.3	39.3/1:36.5
A.A.U.	38.6/1:36.6	35.7/1:33.5	40.7/1:42.0	34.4/1:26.6
Free				
H.S.	32.0/2:16.6	30.6/2:11.1	36.3/2:22.9	29.9/2:06.0
A.A.U.	30.9/2:07.7	28.2/2:00.7	31.7/2:13.7	28.1/1:57.7

The times in the above table are of great interest, but only seven swimmers are involved in the winner's group, and the individual differences are great. The A.A.U. showed much greater proficiency in the breaststroke, but with Jastremski's times in there, this could be expected.

Table II is of greater importance. It gives the percentage

of time spent on each stroke. This comparison provides an opportunity to compare the pace of swimmers with different final times.

Table II
Percentage of time per stroke

Group	Field	Finalists	Last Six	Winners
Fly				
H.S.	20.57	20.51	19.81	20.59
A.A.U.	20.69	21.33	20.41	21.39
Back				
H.S.	25.45	25.73	26.28	24.26
A.A.U.	24.97	25.68	25.48	25.67
Breast				
H.S.	30.61	30.55	30.88	31.20
A.A.U.	30.34	29.62	30.35	29.26
Free				
H.S.	23.41	23.35	24.77	23.70
A.A.U.	24.15	23.34	24.00	21.03

The comparisons in Table II indicate the major error of the slower swimmers. The last six of each group spends less time swimming 'fly in relationship with the final time than any other group. Actually, there is 1.8 per cent difference between them and the winners. In a 2:20.0-200 I.M. this amounts to over 2.5 seconds. It is interesting to note that the percentage of time spent in the freestyle by the 18 High School finalists and the 24 A.A.U. were 23.35 and 23.34 respectively, only 1/100 per cent.

It is from this table the final chart was made. The formula showing the following percentage of time for each stroke was used: 21% - 25% - 30% - 24%. These figures are not the absolute figures that could be used, but disregarding fractions, they are easy to remember and put to use.

Chart III shows the approximate amount of time to be spent on each stroke to do the desired final time. Many observations on this chart, and the others, could be made. The author would welcome all comments.

CHART III

Pace Chart 200 yards Individual Medley

Fly	Back	Breast	Free	Time
25.2	30.0/ 55.2	36.0/1:31.2	28.8 =	2:00.0
26.3	31.3/ 57.6	37.5/1:35.1	30.0 =	2:05.0
27.3	32.5/ 59.8	39.0/1:38.8	31.2 =	2:10.0
27.5	32.8/1:00.3	39.3/1:39.6	31.4 =	2:11.0
27.7	33.0/1:00.7	39.6/1:40.3	31.7 =	2:12.0
27.9	33.3/1:01.2	39.9/1:41.1	31.9 =	2:13.0
28.1	33.5/1:01.6	40.2/1:41.8	32.2 =	2:14.0
28.4	33.7/1:02.1	40.5/1:42.6	32.4 =	2:15.0
28.6	34.0/1:02.6	40.8/1:43.4	32.6 =	2:16.0
28.8	34.3/1:03.1	41.1/1:44.2	32.8 =	2:17.0
28.9	34.5/1:03.4	41.4/1:44.8	33.2 =	2:18.0
29.2	34.7/1:03.9	41.7/1:45.6	33.4 =	2:19.0
29.4	35.0/1:04.4	42.0/1:46.4	33.6 =	2:20.0
29.6	35.3/1:04.9	42.3/1:47.2	33.8 =	2:21.0
29.8	35.5/1:05.3	42.6/1:47.9	34.1 =	2:22.0
30.0	35.8/1:05.8	42.9/1:48.7	34.3 =	2:23.0
30.2	36.0/1:06.2	43.2/1:49.4	34.6 =	2:24.0
30.2	36.3/1:06.8	43.5/1:50.3	34.7 =	2:25.0
30.7	36.5/1:07.2	43.8/1:51.0	35.0 =	2:26.0
30.9	36.8/1:07.7	44.1/1:51.8	35.2 =	2:27.0
31.1	37.0/1:08.1	44.4/1:52.5	35.5 =	2:28.0
31.3	37.3/1:08.6	44.7/1:53.3	35.7 =	2:29.0
31.5	37.5/1:09.0	45.0/1:54.0	36.0 =	2:30.0
31.7	37.7/1:09.4	45.3/1:54.7	36.3 =	2:31.0
31.9	38.0/1:09.9	45.6/1:55.5	36.5 =	2:32.0
32.1	38.3/1:10.4	45.9/1:56.3	36.7 =	2:33.0
32.3	38.5/1:10.8	46.2/1:57.0	37.0 =	2:34.0
32.5	38.7/1:11.2	46.5/1:57.7	37.3 =	2:35.0
32.7	39.0/1:11.7	46.8/1:58.5	37.5 =	2:36.0
32.9	39.2/1:12.1	47.0/1:59.1	37.9 =	2:37.0
33.1	39.5/1:12.6	47.4/2:00.0	38.0 =	2:38.0
33.4	39.7/1:13.1	47.7/2:00.8	38.2 =	2:39.0
33.8	40.0/1:13.8	48.0/2:01.6	38.4 =	2:40.0

Appendix I

World Progressive Best Performances (World Records)

World Best Performances over 220 yards I.M. (Men)
Long Course (55 yards)

2:31.60 John House, U.S.A., Redding, July 19, 1959
2:29.10 John McGill, U.S.A., New London, July 2, 1960
2:24.50 Edward (Ted) Stickles, U.S.A., Fort Lauderdale, Dec. 29, 1960
2:21.80 Edward (Ted) Stickles, U.S.A., Fort Lauderdale, Dec. 29, 1961
2:16.70 Edward (Ted) Stickles, U.S.A. Louisville, July 13, 1962

Long Course (55 yards) Progressive World Best Performances
over 220 yards I.M. (Women)

2:43.20 Sylvia Ruuska, U.S.A., Fresno, Aug. 16, 1958
2:40.30 Sylvia Ruuska, U.S.A., Hobart, Jan. 14, 1959
2:40.10 Donna De Varona, U.S.A., Redding, May 13, 1961
2:39.60 Marguerite Ruygrok, Australia, Sydney, Jan. 2, 1963 (prelim time)
2:38.20 Linda McGill, Australia, Townsville, Sept. 14, 1964
2:36.70 Kendis Moore, U.S.A., Phoenix, July 1965
2:33.90 Claudia Kolb, U.S.A., Cardiff, Aug. 21, 1965 (34.00; 1:15.20; 1:59.80)
2:33.30 Elaine Tanner, Canada, Vancouver, July 3, 1966 (31:10; 1:09.40; 1:57.80)
2:32.00 Elaine Tanner, Canada, Vancouver, Aug. 27, 1966 (1:09.10)
2:32.00 Karen Muir, South Africa, Vancouver, Aug. 27, 1966 (1:11.10)
2:32.00 Shelagh Ratcliffe, England, Blackpool, May 16, 1970

World Progressive Bests 440 yards I.M. (Men)
(55 yards Pools)

5:08.80 Ian Black, Great Britain, Cardiff, June 6, 1959 (1:10.50; 2:34.50; 4:02.80)
5:06.20 Edward (Ted) Stickles, U.S.A., Fresno, Aug. 14, 1960
4:57.10 Edward (Ted) Stickles, U.S.A., Fresno, Aug. 24, 1961
4:51.00 Edward (Ted) Stickles, U.S.A., Louisville, July 12, 1962
4:50.80 Peter Reynolds, Australia, Kingston, Aug. 8, 1966 (1:06.10; 2:17.00; 3:45.70)
4:46.80 Michael Holthaus, West Germany, London, Aug. 20, 1968 (1:02.30; 2:14.50; 3:40.60)

World Progressive Performances over 440 yards I.M. (Women)

5:52.50 Shelly Mann, U.S.A., Tyler, July 5, 1956
5:49.10 Lenie De Nijs, Holland, Durban, Mar. 8–9, 1958
5:46.90 Sylvia Ruuska, U.S.A., Culver City, Aug. 1, 1958
5:41.10 Sylvia Ruuska, U.S.A., Melbourne, Feb. 24, 1959 (1:15.40; 2:43.60; 4:24.20)
5:40.20 Sylvia Ruuska, U.S.A., Redding, July 17, 1959
5:37.90 Donna De Varona, U.S.A., Blackpool, Aug. 26, 1961 (1:16.10; 2:39.50; 4:24.30)
5:30.00 Donna De Varona, U.S.A., Redding, July 1, 1962
5:25.10 Mary Ellen Olcese, U.S.A., Cardiff, Aug. 21, 1965 (1:11.90; 2:32.30; 4:09.9)
5:20.20 Karen Muir, South Africa, Capetown, Feb. 1969
5:19.60 Susan Hunter, New Zealand, 1972

(The above performances no longer recognized for World Record purposes)

200 Metres I.M. (Men). Progressive World Records

2:29.10 Frank Brunell, U.S.A., Akron, July 19, 1958
2:26.20 Lance Larson, U.S.A., Rosemead, Feb. 27, 1960
2:26.20 Gary Heinrich, U.S.A., Los Angeles, June 24–27, 1960
2:22.20 (prelim time) John McGill, U.S.A., Toledo, July 23, 1960
2:22.10 Edward (Ted) Stickles, U.S.A., July 23, 1960
2:21.30 Edward (Ted) Stickles, U.S.A., Chicago, July 2, 1961

2:20.50   Edward (Ted) Stickles, U.S.A., Akron, July 22, 1961

2:19.60   (prelim time) Edward (Ted) Stickles, U.S.A., Los Angeles, Aug. 19, 1961

2:15.90   Edward (Ted) Stickles, U.S.A., Los Angeles, Aug. 19, 1961 (28:20; 1:02.80; 1:42.90)

2:15.50   Richard (Dick) Roth, U.S.A., Los Altos, Aug. 2, 1964 (1:03.90)

2:14.90   Richard (Dick) Roth, U.S.A., Maumee, Aug. 15, 1965 (1:04.10)

2:13.10   Greg Buckingham, U.S.A., Los Altos, July 24, 1966 (28.60; 1:02.40; 1:42.80)

2:12.40   Greg Buckingham, U.S.A., Lincoln, Aug. 21, 1966 (28:30; 1:01.20; 1:42.00)

2:11.30   Greg Buckingham, U.S.A., Oak Park, Aug. 13, 1967 (28.40; 1:02.10; 1:41.10)

2:10.57   Charles Hickcox, U.S.A., Long Beach, Aug. 31, 1968 (27.40; 58.80; 1:40.50)

2:09.60   Gary Hall, U.S.A., Louisville, Aug. 17, 1969 (28.00; 58.90; 1:40.50)

2:09.48   Gary Hall, U.S.A., Los Angeles, Aug. 23, 1970

2:09.30   Gunnar Larsson, Sweden, Barcelona, Sept. 12, 1970 (28.00; 1:00.90; 1:39.50)

2:09.30   Gary Hall, U.S.A., Chicago, Aug. 6, 1972 (26.80; 58.32; 1:39.00)

2:07.17   Gunnar Larsson, Sweden, Munich, Sept. 3, 1972 (28.00; 1:01.07; 1:38.07)

Progressive World Records 200 Metres I.M. Women (Long Course) (50 metres)

2:47.70   Becky Collins, U.S.A., Akron, July 18–20, 1958

2:43.20y   Sylvia Ruuska, U.S.A., Fresno, Aug. 16, 1958

2:40.30y   Sylvia Ruuska, U.S.A., Hobart, Jan. 14, 1959

2:40.10y   Donna De Varona, U.S.A., Redding, May 13, 1961

2:37.20   Donna De Varona, U.S.A., Tenri, July 9, 1961

2:35.00   Donna De Varona, U.S.A., Philadelphia, Aug. 12, 1961 (32.20; 1:10.60)

2:33.30   Donna De Varona, U.S.A., Chicago, Aug. 18, 1962

2:31.80   Donna De Varona, U.S.A., Los Angeles, July 27, 1963 (1:09.40)

2:31.80   Donna De Varona, U.S.A., High Point, Aug. 16, 1963 (31.70; 1:09.20; 1:57.00)

2:30.10   Donna De Varona, U.S.A., Los Angeles, July 11, 1964 (31.80; 1:09.80; 1:55.40)

2:29.90   Donna De Varona, U.S.A., Los Altos, Aug. 1, 1964 (32.70; 1:09.30; 1:55.60)

2:29.00   Lynn Vidali, U.S.A., Los Altos, July 22, 1966

2:28.00   Claudia Kolb, U.S.A., Los Angeles, July 31, 1966 (31.80; 1:10.90; 1:54.00)

2:27.80   Claudia Kolb, U.S.A., Lincoln, Aug. 21, 1966 (32.20; 1:10.60; 1:54.10)

2:27.50   Claudia Kolb, U.S.A., Santa Clara, July 10, 1967 (1:10.40)

2:26.06   Claudia Kolb, U.S.A., Winnipeg, July 30, 1967 (31.40; 1:08.50; 1:51.00)

2:25.00   Claudia Kolb, U.S.A., Philadelphia, Aug. 18, 1967 (31.40; 1:08.60; 1:50.80)

2:25.00   Susan Pedersen, U.S.A., Santa Clara, July 5, 1968 (31.70; 1:10.00; 1:54.70)

2:23.50   Claudia Kolb (actually electronic 2:23.57), U.S.A., Los Angeles, Aug. 25, 1968 (30.80; 1:08.50; 1:50.80)

2:23.07   Shane Gould, Australia, Munich, Aug. 28, 1972 (31.07; 1:08.46; 1:51.07)

2:23.01   Kornelia Ender, D.D.R., East Berlin, Apr. 14, 1973

2:20.51   Andrea Hubner, D.D.R., Belgrade, Sept. 4, 1973 (1:07.04)

400 Metres Individual Medley World Record Progression Men

5:48.5	O'Neil, Frank	Australia	Sydney	17.1.53
5:43.0	O'Neill, Frank	Australia	Sydney	24.2.53
5:38.7*	Kettesy, Gustav	Hungary	Budapest	24.4.53
5:35.6*	Lucien, Maurice	France	Troyes	24.4.53
5:32.1	Kettesy, Gustav	Hungary	Budapest	26.7.53
5:31.0*	Andsberg, Jan	Sweden	Lund	29.10.53
5:27.3	Lucien, Maurice	France	Reims	18.3.54
5:18.3*	Splengler, Alfred	E. Germany	Dresden	22.4.54
5:15.4*	Stroujanov, Vladimir	U.S.S.R.	Minsk	2.10.54
5:09.4*	Androssov, Gennadi	U.S.S.R.	Lvov	10.3.57
5:08.3*	Stroujanov, Vladimir	U.S.S.R.	Moscow	17.3.57

5:15.60   Gary Heinrich, U.S.A., Philadelphia, Aug. 2, 1957

5:12.90   Vladimir Stroujanov, U.S.S.R., Moscow, Oct. 20, 1957

5:08.80y Ian Black, Great Britain, Cardiff, June 6, 1959 (1:10.50; 2:34.50; 4:02.80)

5:07.80 George Harrison, U.S.A., Los Angeles, June 24, 1960 (prelim)

5:05.30 George Harrison, U.S.A., Los Angeles, June 24, 1960

5:04.50 Dennis Rounsavelle, U.S.A., Toledo, July 22, 1960

5:04.30 Edward (Ted) Stickles, U.S.A., Chicago, July 1, 1961

4:56.80 Edward (Ted) Stickles, U.S.A., Cuyahoga Falls, July 21, 1961

4:55.60 Edward (Ted) Stickles, U.S.A., Los Angeles, Aug. 18, 1961 (1:07.10; 2:22.50; 3:47.20)

4:53.80 Gerhard Hetz, West Germany, Moscow, May 24, 1962 (1:04.70; 2:20.60; 3:48.30)

4:51.40 Edward (Ted) Stickles, U.S.A., Chicago, June 30, 1962

4:51.00y Edward (Ted) Stickles, U.S.A., Louisville, July 12, 1962

4:50.20 Gerhard Hetz, West Germany, Tokyo, Oct. 12, 1963 (1:03.70; 2:19.20; 3:44.00)

4:48.60 Richard (Dick) Roth, U.S.A., Los Altos, July 31, 1964 (1:04.60; 2:19.40; 3:44.40)

4:45.40 Richard (Dick) Roth, U.S.A., Tokyo, Oct. 14, 1964 (1:04.10; 2:16.40; 3:41.30)

4:45.30 Andrei Dunaev, U.S.S.R., Tallin, Apr. 3, 1968

4:45.10 Greg Buckingham, U.S.A., Santa Clara, July 6, 1968 (1:02.00; 2:17.10; 3:42.00)

4:43.40 Gary Hall, U.S.A., Los Angeles, July 20, 1968 (1:01.10; 2:13.70; 3:41.00)

4:43.35 (prelim) Charles Hickcox, U.S.A., Long Beach, Aug. 30, 1968 (1:00.0; 2:10.80; 3:39.00)

4:39.00 (actually electronic 4:38.91), Charles Hickcox, U.S.A., Long Beach, Aug. 30, 1968 (59.60; 2:10.40; 3:36.10)

4:38.70 Gary Hall, U.S.A., Santa Clara, July 12, 1969 (1:02.80; 2:13.00; 3:36.70)

4:33.90 Gary Hall, U.S.A., Louisville, Aug. 15, 1969 (1:01.00; 2:08.90; 3:32.60)

4:31.03 Gary Hall, U.S.A., Los Angeles, Aug. 21, 1970 (59.74; 2:07.45; 3:30.24)

4:30.81 Gary Hall, U.S.A., Chicago, Aug. 3, 1972 (59.38; 2:07.17; 3:29.55)

World Record Progression for 400 Metres Individual Medley
(Women)

5:50.4*	Szekely, Eva	Hungary	Budapest	10.4.53
5:47.3*	Kok, Mary	Nether- lands	Hilversum	28.3.55
5:40.8*	Szekely, Eva	Hungary	Budapest	13.7.55
5:38.9*	Kok, Mary	Nether- lands	Hilversum	2.12.56

- -

5:46.60   Sylvia Ruuska, U.S.A., Los Angeles, June 27, 1958

5:43.70   Sylvia Ruuska, U.S.A., Topeka, Aug. 1, 1958

5:39.40   Sylvia Ruuska, U.S.A., San Francisco, Aug. 23–24, 1958

5:36.50   Donna De Varona, U.S.A., Indianapolis, July 15, 1960

5:34.50   Donna De Varona, U.S.A., Philadelphia, Aug. 11, 1961
(1:12.90; 2:36.30; 4:19.00)

5:29.50   Sharon Finneran, U.S.A., Glendale, May 19, 1962

5:27.40   (prelim) Sharon Finneran, U.S.A., Osaka, July 26, 1962

5:24.70   Donna De Varona, U.S.A., Osaka, July 26, 1962 (prelim)
(1:11.10; 2:33.00; 4:11.80)

5:21.90   Sharon Finneran, U.S.A., Osaka, July 28, 1962 (1:12.20;
2:35.80; 4:11.70)

5:16.50   Donna De Varona, U.S.A., Lima, Mar. 10, 1964

5:14.90   Donna De Varona, U.S.A., New York, Aug. 30, 1964
(32.70; 1:10.80; 1:49.70; 2:29.50; 4:04.00; 4:39.20)

5:11.70   Claudia Kolb, U.S.A., Santa Clara, July 8, 1967
(1:09.20; 2:32.40; 4:01.30)

5:09.68   Claudia Kolb, U.S.A., Winnipeg, Aug. 1, 1967 (1:08.46;
2:29.79; 3:59.46)

5:08.20   Claudia Kolb, U.S.A., Philadelphia, Aug. 19, 1967
(1:08.30; 2:28.80; 3:57.20)

5:05.40   Claudia Kolb, U.S.A., Santa Clara, July 6, 1968
(1:08.00; 2:28.10; 3:54.20)

5:04.70   (actually 5:04.62 electronically), Claudia Kolb, U.S.A.,
Los Angeles, Aug. 24, 1968 (1:08.00; 2:28.70; 3:56.30)

5:02.97   Gail Neall, Australia, Munich, Aug. 31, 1972 (1:08.64;
2:25.33; 3:55.51)

5:01.10   Angela Franke, D.D.R., Utrecht, Aug. 18–19, 1973

4:57.51   Gudrun Wegner, D.D.R., Belgrade, Sept. 6, 1973
(1:06.65; 2:23.98; 3:51.34)

* Set in a pool shorter than 50 metres.
The eras when 'short course' and 'long course only' records were
ratified are separated by dotted lines.

Appendix II
Olympic Records

Men's 200 Metres Individual Medley

| 2:12.0 | Hickcox, Charles | U.S.A. | Mexico | 1968 |
| 2:07.17 | Larsson, Gunnar | Sweden | Munich | 1972 |

Men's 400 Metres Individual Medley

4:45.4	Roth, Dick	U.S.A.	Tokyo	1964
4:48.4	Hickcox, Charles	U.S.A.	Mexico	1968
4:31.98	Larsson, Gunnar	Sweden	Munich	1972

Women's 200 Metres Individual Medley

| 2:24.7 | Kolb, Claudia | U.S.A. | Mexico | 1968 |
| 2:23.07 | Gould, Shane | Australia | Munich | 1972 |

Women's 400 Metres Individual Medley

5:18.7	De Varona, Donna	U.S.A.	Tokyo	1964
5:08.5	Kolb, Claudia	U.S.A.	Mexico	1968
5:02.97	Neall, Gail	Australia	Munich	1972

Appendix III
World Rankings

1954 (First year that world list was kept)

Men

400 metres I.M. (50 metres pool only)

Burwell Jones, U.S.A.	5:29.0
George Harrison, U.S.A.	5:33.9
Tim Jecko, U.S.A.	5:33.9
William Yorzyk, U.S.A.	5:35.3
Robert Mattson, U.S.A.	5:39.7
Peter Rademacher, E. Germany	5:43.9
Robert Barry, Australia	5:48.6
Dieter Reinhardt, E. Germany	5:48.7
Frank McKinney, U.S.A.	5:49.6
Charles Krepp, U.S.A.	5:51.7
Arthur Fujino, U.S.A.	5:51.9
Wallace Wolf, U.S.A.	5:51.9
Hans. J. Reich, E. Ger.	5:52.1
Manuel Sanguily, Cuba	5:55.2
Eugene Adler, U.S.A.	5:55.5

Women

400 metres I.M.

Marie Gillet, U.S.A.	6:06.9
Nancy Simon, U.S.A.	6:09.3
Kay Knapp, U.S.A.	6:14.7
Martha, Phyfe, U.S.A.	6:25.1
Mary Jane Sears, U.S.A.	6:26.4
Carolyn Green, U.S.A.	6:26.6
Eva Marie Ten Elsen, E. Germany	6:26.6
Elizabeth Taylor, U.S.A.	6:26.8
Ardis Vinnecour, U.S.A.	6:28.4
Ivanelle Hoe, U.S.A.	6:30.3
Ann Morrison, U.S.A.	6:31.5
Helen Greenlaw, U.S.A.	6:37.2
Gail Mill, U.S.A.	6:38.2

No lists in the I.M. available until 1957 (I guess not being an Olympic event there was not much point for the event outside of the U.S.A.)

1957

Men

400 metres I.M.

Vladimir Stroujanov, U.S.S.R.	5:12.9
Gary Heinrich, U.S.A.	5:15.5
Bill Barton, U.S.A.	5:24.6
Tim Jecko, U.S.A.	5:24.7
Bill Yorzyk, U.S.A.	5:27.8
Frank Brunell, U.S.A.	5:27.8
Darrell Heinrich, U.S.A.	5:28.3
Hal Coulston, U.S.A.	5:30.0
Murray Garrety, Aus.	5:32.5

No women's list

1958

Men
400 metres I.M.

		No women's list
Gary Heinrich, U.S.A.	5:20.2	
Frank Brunell, U.S.A.	5:20.6	
Lance Larson, U.S.A.	5:26.4	
John Fellows, U.S.A.	5:27.3	
Brian Wilkinson, Aus.	5:27.4	
Hal Coulston, U.S.A.	5:28.0	
Brian Foss, U.S.A.	5:28.0	
Bill Barton, U.S.A.	5:28.8	

1959

Men
400 metres I.M.

		No women's list
Ian Black, Gt. Britain	5:08.8	
Gary Heinrich, U.S.A.	5:13.3	
Bill Barton, U.S.A.	5:14.6	
Dennis Rounsavelle, U.S.A.	5:14.9	
Ted Stickles,. U.S.A.	5:18.0	
Eddie Kin, U.S.A.	5:21.8	
Fred Wolf, U.S.A.	5:22.8	
John Hause, U.S.A.	5:23.6	
Pfiffler, Germany	5:24.7	
Yorsegi, Hungary	5:25.2	

1960

Men
400 metres I.M.

		No women's list
Dennis Rounsavelle, U.S.A.	5:04.5	
Ted Stickles, U.S.A.	5:05.0	
George Harrison, U.S.A.	5:05.3	
Gary Heinrich, U.S.A.	5:05.4	
John Hause, U.S.A.	5:09.3	
Ralph Kendrick, U.S.A.	5:12.5	
Bill Barton, U.S.A.	5:14.0	
Eddie Kin, U.S.A.	5:19.4	
Fred Wolf, U.S.A.	5:22.3	
Frank Brunell, U.S.A.	5:23.3	

1961

Men
400 metres I.M.

Women
400 metres I.M.

Ted Stickles, U.S.A.	4:55.6	Donna De Varona, U.S.A.	5:34.5
Gary Tremewan, U.S.A.	5:01.5	Becky Collins, U.S.A.	5:35.7
Carl Robie, U.S.A.	5:04.4	Sharon Finneran, U.S.A.	5:38.7
Nick Kirby, U.S.A.	5:06.3	Judy de Nijs, Holland	5:39.4

Bill Utley, U.S.A.	5:10.6	Carolyn House, U.S.A.	5:40.7
Roy Saari, U.S.A.	5:16.9	Marian Heemskerk, Holl.	5:40.9
Ken Merten, U.S.A.	5:17.7	Robyn Johnson, U.S.A.	5:41.0
Robert Winters, U.S.A.	5:18.0	Heidi Pechtestein, E. Ger.	5:46.6
Tony Tashnick, U.S.A.	5:18.1	Gail Human, U.S.A.	5:47.1
Jergen Bachman, E. Ger.	5:18.1	Marta Egervari, Hungary	5:50.6

1962

Men
400 metres I.M.

Women
400 metres I.M.

Ted Stickles, U.S.A.	4:51.0	Sharon Finneran, U.S.A.	5:21.9
Gerhard Hetz, W. Ger.	4:53.8	Donna De Varona, U.S.A.	5:24.1
Roy Saari, U.S.A.	4:59.0	Adrie Lasterie, Holland	5:27.8
Shigeo Fukushima, Jap.	5:00.2	Carolyn House, U.S.A.	5:28.4
Bill Utley, U.S.A.	5:00.4	Anita Lonsbrough,	
Gennadi Androsov,		Gt. Britain	5:32.3
U.S.S.R.	5:01.3	Marta Egervari, Hungary	5:33.3
Charles Gantner, U.S.A.	5:01.5	Marian Heemskerk, Holl.	5:33.7
Carl Robie, U.S.A.	5:04.6	Gina Ambrose, U.S.A.	5:35.7
Ken Webb, U.S.A.	5:04.7	Cathy Ferguson, U.S.A.	5:37.8
Jan Jiskoot, Holland	5:05.0	Joan Ferris, U.S.A.	5:39.8

1963

Men
400 metres I.M.

Women
400 metres I.M.

Gerhard Hetz, W. Ger.	4:50.2	Donna De Varona, U.S.A.	5:23.2
Carl Robie, U.S.A.	4:52.8	Sharon Finneran, U.S.A.	5:25.3
Ted Stickles, U.S.A.	4:53.3	Gina Ambrose, U.S.A.	5:26.1
Shigeo Fukushima, Jap.	4:53.7	Carolyn House, U.S.A.	5:28.8
Dick Roth, U.S.A.	4:54.4	Martha Randall, U.S.A.	5:31.2
Ralph Kendricks, U.S.A.	4:55.3	Cathy Ferguson, U.S.A.	5:31.7
Gennadi Androsov,		Adrie Lasteris, Holland	5:34.8
U.S.S.R.	4:58.6	Betty Heukels, Holland	5:35.0
Ken Webb, U.S.A.	4:59.4	Linda McGill, Australia	5:35.2
Bill Utley, U.S.A.	5:01.4	Elizabeth Ljunggren,	
B. Gavrilov, U.S.S.R.	5:02.7	Sweden	5:35.4

1964

Men
400 metres I.M.

Women
400 metres I.M.

Dick Roth, U.S.A.	4:45.4	Donna De Varona, U.S.A.	5:14.9
Roy Saari, U.S.A.	4:47.1	Martha Randall, U.S.A.	5:17.9
Gerhard Hetz, W. Ger.	4:51.0	Sharon Finneran, U.S.A.	5:22.2
Carl Robie, U.S.A.	4:51.4	Cathy Ferguson, U.S.A.	5:23.5
Ken Webb, U.S.A.	4:52.6	Jana Haroun, U.S.A.	5:24.0
Ted Stickles, U.S.A.	4:53.7	Jeanne Hallock, U.S.A.	5:24.7
Frank Bates, U.S.A.	4:55.0	Veronika Holletz, E. Ger.	5:25.6
Bill Utley, U.S.A.	4:56.4	Joan Ferris, U.S.A.	5:26.9
Ralph Kendricks, U.S.A.	4:56.8	Linda McGill, Australia	5:28.4
John Porter, U.S.A.	4:57.3	Carolyn House, U.S.A.	5:28.7
		Claudia Kolb, U.S.A.	5:28.7

1965

Men

200 metres I.M.

Dick Roth, U.S.A.	2:14.9
Frank Bates, U.S.A.	2:16.1
Ralph Kendricks, U.S.A.	2:16.3
Bill Utley, U.S.A.	2:17.8
Ed Bettendorf, U.S.A.	2:18.5
Frank Wiegand, E. Ger.	2:18.7
Bob Hopper, U.S.A.	2:19.5
Ken Wiebeck, U.S.A.	2:19.7
Dave Johnson, U.S.A.	2:19.8
Shigeo Fukushima, Jap.	2:20.1

400 metres I.M.

Dick Roth, U.S.A.	4:40.2
Ralph Kendricks, U.S.A.	4:52.7
Frank Bates, U.S.A.	4:54.3
Sandy Gilchrist, Canada	4:55.3
Carl Robie, U.S.A.	4:55.3
Bill Utley, U.S.A.	4:56.2
Frank Wiegand, E. Ger.	4:56.7
Phil Houser, U.S.A.	4:57.5
Andrei Dunaev, U.S.S.R.	4:57.8
Oleg Fotin, U.S.S.R.	4:58.3

Women

200 metres I.M.

Claudia Kolb, U.S.A.	2:30.8
Judy Humbarger, U.S.A.	2:30.9
Jana Haroun, U.S.A.	2:32.1
Cindy Kane, U.S.A.	2:32.9
Martha Randall, U.S.A.	2:33.7
Jane Barkman, U.S.A.	2:34.1
Jeanne Hallock, U.S.A.	2:34.3
Veronika Holletz, E. Ger.	2:34.4
Pokey Watson, U.S.A.	2:35.8
Judy Reeder, U.S.A.	2:36.1

400 metres I.M.

Mary Ellen Olcese, U.S.A.	5:19.6
Patty Carreto, U.S.A.	5:23.0
Jana Haroun, U.S.A.	5:24.0
Martha Randall, U.S.A.	5:24.0
Sharon Finneran, U.S.A.	5:24.5
Cathy Ferguson, U.S.A.	5:24.5
Claudia Kolb, U.S.A.	5:26.9
Betty Heukels, Holland	5:28.8
Eva Wittke, E. Ger.	5:30.8
Debby Ledford, U.S.A.	5:31.0

1966

Men

200 metres I.M.

Greg Buckingham, U.S.A.	2:12.4
Dick Roth, U.S.A.	2:14.7
Charles Hickcox, U.S.A.	2:15.0
Tom Johnson, U.S.A.	2:15.5
Frank Bates, U.S.A.	2:16.5
Bill Utley, U.S.A.	2:16.6
Vladimir Shuhalov, U.S.S.R.	2:17.2
Vladimir Kravtchenko, U.S.S.R.	2:17.2
Frank Wiegand, E. Ger.	2:17.5
Andrei Dunaev, U.S.S.R.	2:17.6

400 metres I.M.

Dick Roth, U.S.A.	4:47.4
Frank Wiegand, E. Ger.	4:47.9
Andrei Dunaev, U.S.S.R.	4:48.7
Peter Reynolds, Australia	4:50.8
Ralph Hutton, Canada	4:51.8
Dave Johnson, U.S.A.	4:52.1
Ken Webb, U.S.A.	4:52.4
Bill Utley, U.S.A.	4:53.8
Oleg Fotin, U.S.S.R.	4:54.1
Phil Houser, U.S.A.	4:55.1

Women

200 metres I.M.

Claudia Kolb, U.S.A.	2:27.8
Lynn Vidali, U.S.A.	2:29.0
Maddie Ellis, U.S.A.	2:31.8
Elaine Tanner, Canada	2:32.0
Karen Muir, S. Africa	2:32.0
Martha Randall, U.S.A.	2:33.0
Cindy Kane, U.S.A.	2:33.9
Tatiana Deviatova, U.S.S.R.	2:33.9
Kathy Thomas, U.S.A.	2:34.3
Jane Barkman, U.S.A.	2:34.8

400 metres I.M.

Claudia Kolb, U.S.A.	5:15.5
Debbie Ledford, U.S.A.	5:19.3
Lynn Vidali, U.S.A.	5:20.0
Mary Ellen Olcese, U.S.A.	5:21.9
Judy Humbarger, U.S.A.	5:24.0
Patty Carreto, U.S.A.	5:24.4
Martha Randall, U.S.A.	5:24.7
Betty Heukels, Holland	5:25.0
Heidi Pechstein, E. Ger.	5:26.0
Elaine Tanner, Canada	5:26.3

1967

Men

200 metres I.M.

Greg Buckingham, U.S.A.	2:11.3
Doug Russell, U.S.A.	2:13.2
Frank Wiegand, E. Ger.	2:13.5
Mark Spitz, U.S.A.	2:13.6
Bill Utley, U.S.A.	2:13.7
Ray Rivero, U.S.A.	2:15.1
Charlie Hickcox, U.S.A.	2:15.4
Alain Mosconi, France	2:16.3
Sandy Gilchrist, Canada	2:16.6
Vladimir Kravtchenko, U.S.S.R.	2:16.9

400 metres I.M.

Peter Williams, U.S.A.	4:46.7
Andrei Dunaev, U.S.S.R.	4:47.2
Bill Utley, U.S.A.	4:48.1
Ken Webb, U.S.A.	4:50.9
John Ferris, U.S.A.	4:52.3
Phil Houser, U.S.A.	4:52.8
Dave Johnson, U.S.A.	4:53.7
Andy Strenk, U.S.A.	4:54.3
Alan Kimber, Gt. Britain	4:54.5
Hans Ljungberg, Swe.	4:54.6

Women

200 metres I.M.

Claudia Kolb, U.S.A.	2:25.0
Sue Pedersen, U.S.A.	2:26.9
Lynn Vidali, U.S.A.	2:27.7
Catie Ball, U.S.A.	2:30.2
Cathy Thomas, U.S.A.	2:30.2
Jane, Barkman, U.S.A.	2:30.5
Cathy Corcione, U.S.A.	2:30.8
Maddie Ellis, U.S.A.	2:31.3
Debbie Ledford, U.S.A.	2:31.9
Sabine Steinbach, E. Ger.	2:32.0

400 metres I.M.

Claudia Kolb, U.S.A.	5:08.2
Sue Pedersen, U.S.A.	5:15.4
Lynn Vidali, U.S.A.	5:17.2
Catie Ball, U.S.A.	5:18.2
Debbie Mayer, U.S.A.	5:19.7
Debbie Ledford, U.S.A.	5:21.1
Mary Ellen Olcese, U.S.A.	5:22.2
Sabine Steinbach, E. Ger.	5:22.6
Judy Humbarger, U.S.A.	5:26.8
Marianne Seidel, E. Ger.	5:27.0

1968: Men's 200 Metres Individual Medley

2:10.6	Hickcox, Charles	U.S.A.	Long Beach	31.8.68
2:11.6	Ferris, John	U.S.A.	Long Beach	31.8.68
2:12.4	Buckingham, Greg	U.S.A.	Long Beach	31.8.68
2:13.6	Williams, Pete	U.S.A.	Long Beach	31.8.68
2:13.7	Bello, Juan	Peru	Mexico City	20.10.68
2:13.9	Johnson, William	U.S.A.	Long Beach	31.8.68
2:13.9	Halthaus, Michael	W. Germany	Berlin	29.8.68
2:13.9	Matthes, Roland	E. Germany	Leipzig	18.8.68
2:13.9	Russell, Doug	U.S.A.	Santa Clara	5.7.68
2:14.5	Hall, Gary	U.S.A.	Long Beach	31.8.68
2:14.5	Johnson, Dave	U.S.A.	Long Beach	31.8.68

1968: Men's 400 Metres Individual Medley

4:39.0	Hickcox, Charles	U.S.A.	Long Beach	30.8.68
4:40.2	Buckingham, Greg	U.S.A.	Long Beach	30.8.68
4:40.6	Hall, Gary	U.S.A.	Long Beach	30.8.68
4:41.8	Williams, Peter	U.S.A.	Long Beach	30.8.68
4:44.0	Holthaus, Michael	W. Germany	Berlin	30.8.68
4:45.3	Ferris, John	U.S.A.	Long Beach	30.8.68
4:45.3	Dunaev, Andrei	U.S.S.R.		
4:48.1	Johnson, Dave	U.S.A.	Long Beach	30.8.68
4:48.1	Strenk, Andy	U.S.A.	Long Beach	30.8.68
4:48.2	McKee, Mark	U.S.A.	Long Beach	30.8.68

1968: Women's 200 Metres Individual Medley

2:23.5	Kolb, Claudia	U.S.A.	Los Angeles	25.8.68
2:25.0	Pedersen, Sue	U.S.A.	Santa Clara	5.7.68
2:25.5	Henne, Jan	U.S.A.	Los Angeles	25.8.68
2:25.6	Vidali, Lynn	U.S.A.	Los Angeles	25.8.68
2:28.4	Corcione, Cathy	U.S.A.	Los Angeles	25.8.68
2:28.9	Ball, Catie	U.S.A.	Fort Lauderdale	20.7.68
2:29.0	Thomas, Kathy	U.S.A.	Lincoln	4.8.68
2:29.6	Turoczy, Judith	Hungary	Budapest	14.7.68
2:30.1	Zakarova, Larissa	U.S.S.R.	Tallin	4.4.68
2:30.3	Watt, Roberta	U.S.A.		

1968: Women's 400 Metres Individual Medley

5:04.7	Kolb, Claudia	U.S.A.	Los Angeles	24.8.68
5:10.3	Pedersen, Sue	U.S.A.	Lincoln	2.8.68
5:12.5	Vidali, Lynn	U.S.A.	Los Angeles	24.8.68
5:14.9	Steinbach, Sabine	E. Germany	Tallin	2.4.68
5:15.1	Thomas, Kathy	U.S.A.	Los Angeles	24.8.68
5:16.1	Caretto, Patty	U.S.A.	Los Angeles	24.8.68
5:16.3	Ball, Catie	U.S.A.	Fort Lauderdale	20.7.68
5:17.3	Seydel, Marianne	E. Germany	Berlin	16.6.68
5:18.4	Rickard, Diana	Australia	Scarborough	8.9.68
5:18.8	Olcese, Mary	U.S.A.	Los Angeles	24.8.68

1969: Men's 200 Metres Individual Medley

2:09.6	Hall, Gary	U.S.A.	Louisville	17.8.69
2:12.6	Russell, Doug	U.S.A.	Louisville	17.8.69
2:13.0	Bella, Juan	Peru	Louisville	17.8.69
2:13.1	Thomas, Carl	U.S.A.	Louisville	17.8.69
2:13.4	Smith, George	Canada	Pointe Claire	14.8.69
2:13.5	Matthes, Roland	E. Germany		
2:13.7	O'Conner, Pat	U.S.A.	Louisville	18.8.69
2:14.0	Chatfield, Mark	U.S.A.	Louisville	17.8.69
2:14.0	Kravtchenko, Vlad.	U.S.S.R.	Mgdbrg.	18.4.69
2:14.6	Fassnacht, Hans	W. Germany	Wrtzbrg.	23.8.69
2:14.6	Power, Steve	U.S.A.	Louisville	17.8.69

1969: Men's 400 Metres Individual Medley

4:33.9	Hall, Gary	U.S.A.	Louisville	16.8.69
4:42.0	Power, Steve	U.S.A.	Louisville	16.8.69
4:42.5	Fassnacht, Hans	W. Germany	Wrtzbrg.	24.8.69
4:44.4	Sperling, Wolfgang	E. Germany	Leipzig	24.7.69
4:45.1	Pechman, M.	E. Germany	Mgdbrg.	18.4.69
4:45.7	Strenk, Andy	U.S.A.	Louisville	16.8.69
4:45.9	Kinkead, Gary	U.S.A.	Louisville	16.8.69
4:47.4	Thomas, Carl	U.S.A.	Louisville	16.8.69
4:47.8	Dunaev, Andrei	U.S.S.R.	Kharkov	12.7.69
4:48.0	Smith, George	Canada	Pointe Claire	12.8.69

1969: Women's 200 Metres Individual Medley

2:26.2	Vidali, Lynn	U.S.A.	Louisville	16.8.69
2:27.5	Pedersen, Sue	U.S.A.	Louisville	16.8.69
2:27.5	Grunert, Martina	E. Germany	Budapest	23.8.69
2:28.1	Attwood, Susie	U.S.A.	Louisville	16.8.69
2:29.1	Thomas, Kathy	U.S.A.	Louisville	16.8.69
2:30.2	Watt, Roberta	U.S.A.	Santa Clara	13.7.69
2:31.0	Milanina, Lidia	U.S.S.R.	Minsk	21.3.69
2:31.0	Turoczy	Hungary	Leipzig	25.7.69
2:31.1	Nishigawa, Yoshima	Japan	Santa Clara	13.7.69
2:31.1	Brecht, Kim	U.S.A.	Louisville	16.8.69

1969: Women's 400 Metres Individual Medley

5:08.6	Meyer, Debbie	U.S.A.	Louisville	15.8.69
5:09.5	Atwood, Susie	U.S.A.	Louisville	15.8.69
5:13.1	Vidali, Lynn	U.S.A.	Louisville	15.8.69
5:15.9	Colella, Lynn	U.S.A.	Louisville	15.8.69
5:17.2	Plaisted, Cindy	U.S.A.	Louisville	15.8.69
5:17.7	Kiddie, Linda	U.S.A.	Santa Clara	15.8.69
5:18.8	Thomas, Kathy	U.S.A.	Louisville	15.8.69
5:19.8	Nishigawa, Yoshima	Japan	Santa Clara	12.7.69
5:20.2y	Muir, Karen	South Africa	Capetown	21.4.69
5:20.4	King, Vicki	U.S.A.	Louisville	15.8.69

1970: Men's 200 Metres Individual Medley

2:09.3	Larsson, Gunnar	Sweden	Barcelona	12.9.70
2:09.5	Hall, Gary	U.S.A.	Los Angeles	23.8.70
2:11.7	Ferris, John	U.S.A.	Los Angeles	23.8.70
2:11.8	O'Connor, Pat	U.S.A.	Los Angeles	23.8.70
2:12.5	Furniss, Steve	U.S.A.	Los Angeles	23.8.70
2:12.8	Matthes, Roland	E. Germany	Brndnbrg.	11.7.70
2:12.9	Stamm, Mike	U.S.A.	Los Angeles	23.8.70
2:13.0	Kravachenko, Vlad.	U.S.S.R.	Novsbrsk.	15.8.70
2:13.0	McKee, Tim	U.S.A.	Los Angeles	23.8.70
2:13.3	Chatfield, Mark	U.S.A.	Los Angeles	23.8.70

1970: Men's 400 Metres Individual Medley

4:31.0	Hall, Gary	U.S.A.	Los Angeles	21.8.70
4:36.2	Larsson, Gunnar	Sweden	Barcelona	8.9.70
4:36.9	Fassnacht, Hans	W. Germany	Barcelona	8.9.70
4:38.6	Power, Steve	U.S.A.	Los Angeles	21.8.70
4:39.9	Colella, Rick	U.S.A.	Los Angeles	21.8.70
4:40.6	Pechmann, Mathias	E. Germany	Barcelona	8.9.70
4:41.9	DeRoest, John	U.S.A.	Los Angeles	21.8.70
4:43.5	Holthaus, Michael	W. Germany	Barcelona	8.9.70
4:43.8	Ljungberg, Hans	Sweden	Barcelona	8.9.70
4:44.8	Bahler, David	U.S.A.	Los Angeles	21.8.70

1970: Women's 200 Metres Individual Medley

2:25.8	Nishigawa, Yoshima	Japan	Winnipeg	3.8.70
2:26.0	Vidali, Lynn	U.S.A.	Los Angeles	23.8.70
2:27.0	Watt, Roberta	U.S.A.	Los Angeles	23.8.70
2:27.1	Atwood, Susie	U.S.A.	Los Angeles	23.8.70
2:27.6	Grunert, Martina	E. Germany	Barcelona	9.9.70
2:28.8	Plaisted, Cindy	U.S.A.	Los Angeles	23.8.70
2:28.9	Langford, Denise	Australia	Edinburgh	18.7.70
2:28.9	Wylie, Sara	U.S.A.	Los Angeles	23.8.70
2:29.3	Stolze, Evelyn	E. Germany	Barcelona	8.9.70
2:29.5	Ratcliffe, Sheila	Great Britain	Kecshemet	4.4.70

1970: Women's 400 Metres Individual Medley

5:07.3	Atwood, Susie	U.S.A.	Los Angeles	21.8.70
5:07.9	Stolze, Evelyn	E. Germany	Barcelona	6.9.70
5:08.7	Plaisted, Cindy	U.S.A.	Los Angeles	21.8.70
5:10.7	Langford, Denise	Australia	Edinburgh	21.7.70
5:11.3	Meyer, Debbie	U.S.A.	Los Angeles	21.8.70
5:11.8	Nishigawa, Yoshima	Japan	Winnipeg	1.8.70
5:15.8	Neall, Gail	Australia	Edinburgh	21.7.70
5:16.3	Bartz, Jenny	U.S.A.	Los Angeles	21.8.70
5:16.8	Kiddie, Linda	U.S.A.	Los Angeles	21.8.70
5:17.9	Ratcliffe, Sheila	Great Britain	Edinburgh	21.7.70

1971: Men's 200 Metres Individual Medley

2:09.79	Hall, Gary	U.S.A.	Minsk	9.9.71
2:10.2	Larsson, Gunnar	Sweden	Uppsala	28.8.71
2:10.82	Furniss, Steve	U.S.A.	Cali	9.8.71
2:11.12	McKee, Tim	U.S.A.	Houston	28.8.71
2:11.34	Thomas, Carl	U.S.A.	Houston	28.8.71
2:11.50	O'Connor, Pat	U.S.A.	Houston	28.8.71
2:12.11	Heckl, Frank	U.S.A.	Cali	9.8.71
2:12.3	Shuchavev, Mik.	U.S.S.R.	Uppsala	28.8.71
2:12.32	Colella, Rick	U.S.A.	Minsk	9.9.71
2:12.4	Hargitay, Andras	Hungary	Budapest	11.4.71

1971: Men's 400 Metres Individual Medley

4:33.11	Hall, Gary	U.S.A.	Houston	26.8.71
4:34.88	Colella, Rick	U.S.A.	Houston	26.8.71
4:36.90	McKee, Tim	U.S.A.	Houston	26.8.71
4:38.8	Larsson, Gunnar	Sweden	Uppsala	29.8.71
4:40.24	Furniss, Steve	U.S.A.	Houston	26.8.71
4:40.48	Fassnacht, Hans	W. Germany	Houston	26.8.71
4:40.5	Windeatt, Graham	Australia	S.C.S.C.	10.7.71
4:40.6	Hargitay, Andras	Hungary	Budapest	11.4.71
4:40.6	Power, Steve	U.S.A.	Houston	26.8.71
4:40.9	Pechmann, Matthias	E. Germany	Uppsala	29.8.71

1971: Women's 200 Metres Individual Medley

2:25.62	Nishigawa, Yoshima	Japan	Houston	28.8.71
2:26.67	Bartz, Jenny	U.S.A.	Houston	28.8.71
2:26.98	Cliff, Leslie	Canada	Houston	28.8.71
2:27.78	Montgomery, Mary	U.S.A.	Houston	28.8.71
2:28.0	Slavickova, Jar.	Czech.	Berlin	14.7.71
2:28.04	Plaisted, Cindy	U.S.A.	Houston	28.8.71
2:28.5	Atwood, Sue	U.S.A.	Leipzig	4.9.71
2:28.7	Cain, Debbie	Australia	London	1.5.71
2:29.2	Gould, Shane	Australia	Hobart	5.2.71
2:29.7	Turoczy, Judit	Hungary	Budapest	

1971: Women's 400 Metres Individual Medley

5:07.9	Plaisted, Cindy	U.S.A.	S.C.S.C.	10.7.71
5:08.1	Moras, Karen	Australia	S.C.S.C.	10.7.71
5:08.38	Bartz, Jenny	U.S.A.	Houston	26.8.71
5:09.3	Gould, Shane	Australia	Sydney	11.12.71
5:10.22	Cliff, Leslie	Canada	Houston	26.8.71
5:10.37	Atwood, Sue	U.S.A.	Houston	26.8.71
5:11.78	Nishigawa, Yoshima	Japan	Houston	26.8.71
5:13.17	Block, Terry	U.S.A.	Houston	26.8.71
5:13.52	Enze, Cindy	U.S.A.	Houston	26.8.71
5:13.85	Hubbart, Joan	U.S.A.	Houston	26.8.71

1972: Men's 200 Metres Individual Medley

2:07.17	Larsson, Gunnar	Sweden	Munich	3.9.72
2:08.37	McKee, Tim	U.S.A.	Munich	3.9.72
2:08.45	Furniss, Steve	U.S.A.	Munich	3.9.72
2:08.49	Hall, Gary	U.S.A.	Munich	3.9.72
2:09.66	Hargitay, Andras	Hungary	Munich	3.9.72
2:09.90	Tyler, Fred	U.S.A.	Chicago	6.8.72
2:10.17	Thomas, Carl	U.S.A.	Chicago	6.8.72
2:10.63	Carper, Stan	U.S.A.	Chicago	6.8.72
2:10.96	O'Connor, Pat	U.S.A.	Chicago	6.8.72
2:11.10	Sperling, Wolfram	E. Germany	Leipzig	11.7.72

1972: Men's 400 Metres Individual Medley

4:30.81	Hall, Gary	U.S.A.	Santa Clara	24.6.72
4:31.98	Larsson, Gunnar	Sweden	Munich	30.8.72
4:31.98	McKee, Tim	U.S.A.	Munich	30.8.72
4:32.70	Hargitay, Andras	Hungary	Munich	30.8.72
4:34.92	Furniss, Steve	U.S.A.	Chicago	3.8.72
4:36.21	Colella, Rick	U.S.A.	Chicago	3.8.72
4:36.76	Power, Steve	U.S.A.	Chicago	3.8.72
4:37.96	Gingsjo, Bengt	Sweden	Munich	30.8.72
4:38.90	Sperling, Wolfram	E. Germany	Leipzig	8.7.72
4:39.30	Suharev, Mikhail	U.S.S.R.	Moscow	4.8.72

1972: Women's 200 Metres Individual Medley

2:23.07	Gould, Shane	Australia	Munich	28.8.72
2:23.59	Ender, Kornelia	E. Germany	Munich	28.8.72
2:24.06	Vidali, Lynn	U.S.A.	Munich	28.8.72
2:24.51	Woods, Carolyn	U.S.A.	Chicago	2.8.72
2:24.55	Bartz, Jenny	U.S.A.	Munich	28.8.72
2:24.83	Cliff, Leslie	Canada	Munich	28.8.72
2:26.35	Nishigawa, Yoshima	Japan	Munich	28.8.72
2:26.66	Atwood, Susie	U.S.A.	Chicago	2.8.72
2:26.80	Petrova, Nina	U.S.S.R.	Hanover	18.4.72
2:27.14	Montgomery, Mary	U.S.A.	Chicago	2.8.72

1972: Women's 400 Metres Individual Medley

5:02.97	Neall, Gail	Australia	Munich	31.8.72
5:03.57	Cliff, Leslie	Canada	Munich	31.8.72
5:03.99	Calligaris, Novella	Italy	Munich	31.8.72
5:04.96	Montgomery, Mary	U.S.A.	Chicago	4.8.72
5:02.26	Bartz, Jenny	U.S.A.	Chicago	4.8.72
5:06.80	Stolze, Evelyn	E. Germany	Munich	31.8.72
5:07.40	Gould, Shane	Australia	Sydney	8.1.72
5:07.64	Vidali, Lynn	U.S.A.	Chicago	4.8.72
5:07.80	Block, Terri	U.S.A.	Santa Clara	23.7.72
5:11.40	Rothhammer, Keena	U.S.A.	Santa Clara	4.6.72

1973: Men's 200 Metres Individual Medley

2:08.36	Larsson, Gunnar	Sweden	Belgrade	7.9.73
2:08.43	Carper, Stan	U.S.A.	Belgrade	7.9.73
2:08.78	Furniss, Steve	U.S.A.	Los Angeles	2.8.73
2:08.84	Wilkie, David	Great Britain	Belgrade	7.9.73
2:09.50	Colella, Rick	U.S.A.	Crys. Pal.	23.4.73
2:09.52	Hargitay, Andras	Hungary	Belgrade	7.9.73
2:09.57	Leitzman, Chris	E. Germany	Belgrade	7.9.73
2:09.65	Brown, Scott	U.S.A.	Lousiville	26.8.73
2:10.06	Pytell, Roger	E. Germany	Berlin	15.7.73
2:10.07	Tyler, Fred	U.S.A.	Louisville	26.8.73
2:10.54	Sperling, Wolfram	E. Germany	Belgrade	7.9.73
2:10.82	Hencken, John	U.S.A.	Louisville	26.8.73
2:10.86	Zakarov, Sergei	U.S.S.R.	Belgrade	7.9.73
2:10.95	Brinkley, Brian	Great Britain	Coventry	2.8.73
2:11.36	Szuba, Tom	U.S.A.	Louisville	26.8.73
2:11.67	Sukharev, Mikhail	U.S.S.R.	Berlin	14.4.73
2:11.72	Backhaus, Robin	U.S.A.	Louisville	26.8.73
2:11.82	Hannula, Dave	U.S.A.	Louisville	26.8.73
2:11.98	Smirnov, Andrei	U.S.S.R.	Belgrade	7.9.73
2:12.20	Verrastto, Zoltan	Hungary	Budapest	3.8.73
2:12.60	Poucher, Allen	U.S.A.	Fort Lauderdale	14.7.73
2:12.70	Brumwell, Dave	Canada	Laval	25.7.73

2:12.77	Lautman, Scott	U.S.A.	Louisville	26.8.73
2:13.00	Terrell, Ray	Great Britain	Coventry	2.8.73
2:13.03	Furniss, Bruce	U.S.A.	Louisville	26.8.73

1973: Men's 400 Metres Individual Medley

4:31.11	Hargitay, Andras	Hungary	Belgrade	5.9.73
4:32.38	Colella, Rick	U.S.A.	Louisville	23.8.73
4:33.50	Strachan, Rod	U.S.A.	Belgrade	5.9.73
4:36.29	Brinkley, Brian	Great Britain	Coventry	4.8.73
4:36.63	Furniss, Steve	U.S.A.	Los Angeles	3.8.73
4:36.80	Szuba, Tom	U.S.A.	Louisville	23.8.73
4:37.05	Hannula, Dave	U.S.A.	Louisville	23.8.73
4:37.05	Zakarov, Sergei	U.S.S.R.	Belgrade	5.9.73
4:37.17	Sperling, Wolfram	E. Germany	Belgrade	5.9.73
4:37.33	Brown, Scott	U.S.A.	Louisville	23.8.73
4:37.62	Gingsjoe, Bengt	Sweden	Belgrade	5.9.73
4:38.81	Lautman, Scott	U.S.A.	Santa Clara	23.6.73
4:40.13	Engstrand, Lee	U.S.A.	Moscow	22.8.73
4:40.50	Lietzman, Chris	E. Germany	Berlin	11.7.73
4:40.60	Smirnov, Andre	U.S.S.R.	Rostov	2.17.73
4:40.62	DeMont, Rick	U.S.A.	Louisville	23.8.73
4:42.28	Dickson, Bruce	U.S.A.	Louisville	23.8.73
4:42.59	Sukharev, Mikhail	U.S.S.R.	Moscow	22.8.73
4:43.00	Verraszto, Zoltan	Hungary	Budapest	2.8.73
4:43.10	Hochstrasser, Tye	U.S.A.	Louisville	23.8.73
4:43.40	Martin, Neil	Australia	Queensland	13.1.73
4:43.51	Delgado, Jorge	Ecuador	Rio	22.4.73
4:43.88	Henry, Shafer	U.S.A.	Louisville	23.8.73
4:44.00	Moreau, Patrick	France	Berlin	18.8.73
4:44.20	Geisler, Hans J.	W. Germany	Bonn	28.7.73

1973: Women's 200 Metres Individual Medley

| 2:20.51 | Huber, Andrea | E. Germany | Belgrade | 4.9.73 |
| 2:21.51 | Ender, Kornelia | E. Germany | Belgrade | 4.9.73 |

2:23.84	Heddy, Kathy	U.S.A.	Belgrade	4.9.73
2:23.90	Gould, Shane	Australia	Crys. Pal.	21.4.73
2:24.07	Calligaris, Novella	Italy	Belgrade	4.9.73
2:24.18	Eife, Andrea	E. Germany	Berlin	12.7.73
2:25.72	Woodcock, Julie	U.S.A.	Belgrade	4.9.73
2:25.90	Cliff, Leslie	Canada	Laval	25.7.73
2:26.07	Tauber, Ulrike	E. Germany	Leeds	9.8.73
2:26.30	Graham, Maryanne	U.S.A.	Los Angeles	2.8.73
2:26.38	Atwood, Susie	U.S.A.	Moscow	22.8.73
2:26.47	Takemoto, Yukari	Japan	Belgrade	4.9.73
2:26.63	Cain, Debbie	Australia	Belgrade	4.9.73
2:26.90	Whitaker, Susie	U.S.A.	Louisville	25.8.73
2:27.10	Bartz, Jenny	U.S.A.	Louisville	15.8.73
2:27.58	Branman, Robin	U.S.A.	Louisville	25.8.73
2:27.77	Herbst, Christine	E. Germany	Berlin	13.4.73
2:27.80	Hinze, Petra	E. Germany	T'jabius	13.4.73
2:27.84	Franks, Jenny	U.S.A.	Louisville	25.8.73
2:27.91	Pohl, Marlies	E. Germany	Berlin	13.4.73
2:28.03	Walsh, Huddie	U.S.A.	Louisville	25.8.73
2:28.30	Petrova, Nina	U.S.S.R.	Berlin	13.4.73
2:28.65	Carr, Cathy	U.S.A.	Moscow	22.8.73
2:28.69	Smith, Becky	Canada	N. W'ster.	6.8.73
2:28.80	Nazereevw, Wijda	Holland	Utrecht	18.8.73

1973: Women's 400 Metres Individual Medley

4:57.51	Wegner, Gudrun	E. Germany	Belgrade	6.9.73
5:00.37	Franke, Angela	E. Germany	Belgrade	6.9.73
5:02.02	Calligaris, Novella	Italy	Belgrade	6.9.73
5:07.01	Cliff, Leslie	Canada	Belgrade	6.9.73
5:08.01	Gould, Shane	Australia	Santa Clara	23.6.73
5:08.36	Hunter, Susan	N. Zealand	Belgrade	6.9.73
5:08.73	Bartz, Jenny	U.S.A.	Louisville	23.8.73
5:08.74	Atwood, Susie	U.S.A.	Los Angeles	3.8.73
5:09.03	Potts, Terry	U.S.A.	Belgrade	6.9.73

5:10.10	Lockyer, Sally	Australia	D'moyne	7.12.73
5:10.41	McHugh, Jennifer	Canada	Laval	23.7.73
5:10.46	Woodcock, Julie	U.S.A.	Lancaster	4.8.73
5:10.60	Neall, Gail	Australia	Brisbane	5.8.73
5:11.61	Schuchardt, Brigitte	W. Germany	Berlin	12.7.73
5:11.69	Walsh, Huddie	U.S.A.	Louisville	23.8.73
5:12.10	Whitaker, Sue	U.S.A.	Louisville	23.8.73
5:12.17	Damen, Jose	Holland	Belgrade	6.9.73
5:12.24	Graham, Maryanne	U.S.A.	Los Angeles	3.8.73
5:12.40	Hinze, Petra	E. Germany	T'jabisk	14.4.73
5:12.99	Oullette, Kim	U.S.A.	Louisville	23.8.73
5:13.21	Shettle, Kim	U.S.A.	Louisville	23.8.73
5:13.41	Schuetz, Uta	W. Germany	Belgrade	6.9.73
5:13.51	Hogan, Liz	U.S.A.	Louisville	23.8.73
5:13.56	Heddy, Kathy	U.S.A.	Louisville	23.8.73
5:13.80	Belote, Melissa	U.S.A.	Washington	22.7.73
5:13.80	Bengtson, Debbie	Canada	Laval	23.7.73

Appendix IV

◦—◦

Commonwealth Progressive Best Performances over 220 yards I.M. (Men) (55 yards Pool)

2:28.80 William Ebsary, Australia, Melbourne, Oct. 25, 1962
2:28.80 Alex Alexander, Australia, Melbourne, Oct. 25, 1962
2:28.30 Robert Walker, New Zealand, Auckland, Mar. 2, 1963
2:23.30 Ralph Hutton, Canada, Fresno, Aug. 21, 1964
2:22.30 Peter Reynolds, Australia, Hobart, Feb. 27, 1965
2:20.50 Sandy Gilchrist, Canada, Hamilton, July, 1966
2:19.80 Peter Reynolds, Australia, Blackpool, Aug. 12, 1967
2:19.60 Raymond Terrell, England, London, May 4, 1968
2:18.90 Martyn Woodroffe, Wales, Blackpool, Aug. 6–11, 1968
2:17.90 Martyn Woodroffe, Wales, Coventry, May 30–31, 1969
2:17.60 Martyn Woodroffe, Wales, Blackpool, Aug. 4–9, 1969

Commonwealth Progressive Records over 220 yards I.M. (Women) (55 yards Pool)

2:48.40 (prelim time) Dawn Fraser, Australia, Hobart, Jan. 13, 1959
2:44.20 Dawn Fraser, Australia, Hobart, Jan. 14, 1959
2:39.60 (W.R.) Marguerite Ruygrok, Australia, Sydney, Jan. 2, 1963
2:38.20 (W.R.) Linda McGill, Australia, Townsville, Sept. 14, 1964
2:33.30 (W.R.) Elaine Tanner, Canada, Vancouver, July 3, 1966
2:32.00 (W.R.) Elaine Tanner, Canada, Vancouver, Aug. 27, 1966
2:32.00 Shelagh Ratcliffe, England, Blackpool, May 16, 1970

(No longer recognized for World Record performances)

Commonwealth Progressive Best Performances over 440 yards I.M. (Men) (55 yards Pool)

5:27.40 Brian Wilkinson, Australia, Melbourne, Feb. 18, 1958
5:26.30 Alan Kable, Australia, Sydney, Jan. 17, 1959
5:08.80 (W.R.) Ian Black, Scotland, Cardiff, June 6, 1959
5:07.10 (prelim time) Sandy Gilchrist, Canada, Vancouver, Sept. 2, 1964

4:59.20 Sandy Gilchrist, Canada, Vancouver, Sept. 3, 1964
4:55.30 Sandy Gilchrist, Canada, Blackpool, Aug. 12, 1965
4:50.80 (*W.R.*) Peter Reynolds, Australia, Kingston, Aug. 8, 1966

Commonwealth Progressive List for 440 yards I.M. (Women)
(55 yards Pool)

6:04.60 Christine Gosden, England, Cardiff, June 6, 1959
5:54.50 Alva Colquhoun, Australia, Sydney, Feb. 20, 1960
5:54.10 Linda McGill, Australia, Sydney, Dec. 23, 1961
5:42.10 Linda McGill, Australia, Sydney, Jan. 20, 1962
5:39.40 Anita Lonsbrough, England, Blackpool, June 23, 1962
5:38.60 Anita Lonsbrough, Perth, Nov. 30, 1962
5:35.20 Linda McGill, Australia, Sydney, Jan. 8, 1963
5:33.60 Anita Lonsbrough, England, Blackpool, May 30, 1964
5:33.00 Barbara Hounsel, Canada, Vancouver, Sept. 3, 1964
5:30.10 Elaine Tanner, Canada, Vancouver, July, 1966
5:27.20 Elaine Tanner, Canada, Hamilton, July, 1966
5:26.30 Elaine Tanner, Canada, Kingston, Aug. 12, 1966
5:22.80 Shelagh Ratcliffe, England, London, Mar. 14, 1970
5:21.00 Susan Hunter, New Zealand, Christchurch, 1971? 1972?

Commonwealth Progressive Records List for 200 Metres
I.M. (Men)

2:28.80y William Ebsary, Australia, Melbourne, Oct. 25, 1962
2:28.80y Alex Alexander, Australia, Melbourne, Oct. 25, 1962 (finished second to Ebsary)
2:28.30y Robert Walker, New Zealand, Auckland, Mar. 2, 1963
2:24.30 (prelim time) Ian O'Brien, Australia, Sydney, Jan. 17, 1964
2:21.40 Terry Buck, Australia, Sydney, Jan. 18, 1964
2:20.50 Peter Reynolds, Australia, Sydney, Jan. 16, 1965
2:19.20 Peter Reynolds, Australia, Feb. 11, 1966
2:16.91 (prelim time) Sandy Gilchrist, Canada, Winnipeg, July 27, 1967 (1:03.63)
2:16.61 (third place) Sandy Gilchrist, Canada, Winnipeg, July 27, 1967 (1:03.76)
2:16.40 George Smith, Canada, Winnipeg, Aug. 16, 1968 (1:03.50)

2:16.40 (prelim time) George Smith, Canada, Mexico City, Oct. 19, 1968

2:15.90 (fifth place) George Smith, Canada, Mexico City, Oct. 20, 1968

2:13.40 George Smith, Canada, Pointe Claire, Aug. 11–15, 1969

2:11.90 Raymond Terrell, England, London, July 13, 1972

2:10.00 (second) David Wilkie, Scotland, London, Apr. 23, 1973

2:09.61 (prelim) David Wilkie, Scotland, Belgrade, Sept. 7, 1973

2:08.84 (third) David Wilkie, Scotland, Belgrade, Sept. 7, 1973 (1:02.07)

Commonwealth Progressive Records List for 200 Metres
I.M. (Women)

2:48.40y (prelim) Dawn Fraser, Australia, Hobart, Jan. 13, 1959

2:44.20 (second) Dawn Fraser, Australia, Hobart, Jan. 14, 1959

2:39.60y (prelim) Marguerite Ruygrok, Australia, Sydney, Jan. 2, 1963

2:39.00 Linda McGill, Australia, Sydney, Jan. 4, 1964

2:38.20y Linda McGill, Australia, Townsville, Sept. 14, 1964

2:37.90 Jan Murphy, Australia, Sydney, Feb. 11, 1966.

2:33.30y Elaine Tanner, Canada, Vancouver, July 3, 1966 (31.10; 1:09.40; 1:57.80)

2:32.00y Elaine Tanner, Canada, Vancouver, Aug. 27, 1966 (1:09.10)

2:31.80 Elaine Tanner, Canada, Winnipeg, Aug. 16, 1968 (1:08.90)

2:30.90 Dianna Rickard, Australia, Scarborough, Sept. 7, 1968 (33.50; 1:09.80; 1:55.70)

2:29.50 Shelagh Ratcliffe, England, Kecskemet, Apr. 4, 1970

2:28.89 Denise Langford, Australia, Edinburgh, July 18, 1970

2:28.73 (second place) Deborah Caine, Australia, London, Apr. 30, 1971

2:26.98 (third place) Leslie Cliff, Canada, Houston, Aug. 28, 1971 (1:08.98)

2:24.40 Shane Gould, Australia, Sydney, Jan. 15, 1972 (31.50; 1:08.60; 1:52.40)

2:23.07 (*W.R.*) Shane Gould, Australia, Munich, Aug. 28, 1972 (31.07; 1:08.46; 1:51.07)

*Commonwealth Progressive Records List for 400 Metres
I.M. (Long Course) (Men)*

5:27.40y Brian Wilkinson, Australia, Melbourne, Feb. 18, 1958
5:26.30y Alan Kable, Australia, Sydney, Jan. 17, 1959
5:08.80y (*W.R.*) Ian Black, Scotland, Cardiff, June 6, 1959
5:08.80 Sandy Gilchrist, Canada, Montreal, July 24–27, 1963
5:03.70 Alex Alexander, Australia, Sydney, Jan. 22, 1964
4:59.20y Sandy Gilchrist, Canada, Vancouver, Sept. 3, 1964
4:58.30 (prelim) Sandy Gilchrist, Canada, Tokyo, Oct. 12, 1964
4:57.60 (fifth) Sandy Gilchrist, Canada, Tokyo, Oct. 14, 1964
4:55.30y Sandy Gilchrist, Canada, Blackpool, Aug. 12, 1965
4:54.90 Peter Reynolds, Australia, 1966
4:54.00 Peter Reynolds, Australia, Brisbane, Feb. 26, 1966
4:50.80y Peter Reynolds, Australia, Kingston, Aug. 8, 1966
(1:06.10; 2:17.00; 3:45.70)
4:49.50 (fourth) Martyn Woodroffe, Wales, Santa Clara, July 12,
1969 (1:02.50; 2:17.20; 3:44.80)
4:48.00 George Smith, Canada, Pointe Claire, Aug. 11–15, 1969
4:45.26 (second) Graham Windeatt, Australia, London, Apr. 30,
1971
4:42.70 Graham Windeatt, Australia, Hamburg, May 14, 1971
4:40.50 Graham Windeatt, Australia, Santa Clara, July 10, 1971
(1:05.10; 2:16.50; 3:40.60)
4:40.39 (seventh) Graham Windeat, Australia, Munich, Aug. 30,
1972 (1:03.70; 2:15.87; 3:38.76)
4:36.29 Brian Brinkley, England, Coventry, Aug. 4, 1973

*Commonwealth Progressive Records List for 400 Metres
Individual Medley (Long Course) (Women)*

6:04.60y Christine Gosden, England, Cardiff, June 6, 1959
5:54.50y Alva Colquhoun, Australia, Sydney, Feb. 20, 1960
5:54.10y Linda McGill, Australia, Sydney, Dec. 23, 1961
5:42.10y Linda McGill, Australia, Sydney, Jan. 20, 1962
5:39.40y Anita Lonsbrough, England, Blackpool, June 23, 1962
5:37.60 Anita Lonsbrough, England, Budapest, July 8, 1962
5:32.30 (second) Anita Lonsborough, England, Leipzig, Aug.
25, 1962
5:30.60 (prelim time) Anita Lonsbrough, England, Tokyo,
Oct. 15, 1964
5:28.40 (fifth) Linda McGill, Australia, Tokyo, Oct. 17, 1964
5:27.20y Elaine Tanner, Canada, Hamilton, July 1966

5:26.30y Elaine Tanner, Canada, Kingston, Aug. 12, 1966
5:24.70 Shelagh Ratcliffe, England, Stockholm Aprl. 20–21, 1968
5:24.50 Shelagh Ratcliffe, England, Budapest, July 13, 1968
5:21.70 Diana Rickard, Australia, Brisbane, Aug. 24, 1968
5:18.40 Diane Rickard, Australia, Scarborough, Sept. 8, 1968 (1:12.20; 2:31.70; 4:06.20)
5:17.80 Denise Langford, Australia, Drummoyne, Feb. 27, 1970 (1:14.00; 2:35.30; 4:08.60)
5:14.25 (prelim) Denise Langford, Australia, Edinburgh, July 21, 1970
5:10.74 Denise Langford, Australia, Edinburgh, July 23, 1970
5:08.10 (second) Karen Moras, Australia, Santa Clara, July 10, 1971 (1:11.50; 2:30.20; 4:02.00)
5:07.40 Shane Gould, Australia, Sydney, Jan. 9, 1972 (1:09.50; 2:28.50; 4:00.70)
5:02.97 (*W.R.*) Gail Neall, Australia, Munich, Aug. 31, 1972 (1:08.64; 2:25.33; 3:55.51)

Appendix V

—o—o—o—o—o—o—o—o—o—o—o—o—o—o—o—o—o—o—o—o—o—o—o—o—o—o—o—o—o—o—o—o—

European Progressive Records List for 200 Metres I.M.
(Women) (Long Course)

2:44.20 (third) Greta Kok, Holland, Munich, Sept. 3, 1961

2:42.00 Ursel Brunner, West Germany, Dortmund, May 19, 1962

2:39.80 Ursel Brunner, West Germany, Dortmund, May 18, 1963

2:39.00 Harriet Blank, D.D.R., Magdeburg, Feb. 29, 1964

2:37.70 Veronika Holletz, D.D.R., East Berlin, June 21, 1964

2:34.40 Veronika Holletz, D.D.R., East Berlin, Aug. 14, 1965

2:33.90 Tatyana Devyatova, U.S.S.R., Moscow, Aug. 13, 1966

2:33.50 Sabine Steinbach, D.D.R., Karl Marx Stadt, 1967

2:32.00 Sabine Steinbach, D.D.R., Linkoping, Aug. 15, 1967 (31.70; 1:09.80; 1:54.80)

2:31.10 Sabine Steinbach, D.D.R., East Berlin, Mar. 10, 1968

2:30.10 Larissa Zahkarova, U.S.S.R., Tallin, Apr. 3, 1968

2:29.60 Judit Turoczy, Hungary, Budapest, July 14, 1968

2:27.50 Martine Grunert, D.D.R., Budapest, Aug. 23, 1969

2:27.50 Gabriele Wetzko, D.D.R., Dresden, Dec. 19, 1971

2:26.90 Nina Petrova, U.S.S.R., Hanover, Apr. 18, 1972

2:25.45 (prelim) Evelyn Stolze, D.D.R., Munich, Aug. 28, 1972

2:25.39 (prelim) Kornelia Ender, D.D.R., Munich, Aug. 28, 1972

2:23.59 (second) Kornelia Ender, D.D.R., Munich, Aug. 28, 1972 (31.45; 1:07.60; 1:52.03)

2:23.01 (*W.R.*) Kornelia Ender, D.D.R., East Berlin, Apr. 14, 1973

2:20.51 (*W.R.*) Andrea Hubner, D.D.R., Belgrade, Sept. 4, 1973 (1:07.04)

European Progressive Records List for 200 Metres
Individual Medley (Men) (Long Course)

2:22.60 Gerhard Hetz, West Germany, Dortmund, May 19, 1962 (30.80; 1:06.20; 1:49.10)

2:18.00 Gerhard Hetz, West Germany, Dortmund, May 18, 1963

2:17.80 Gerhard Hetz, West Germany, Dortmund, May 23, 1964 (29.60; 1:04.10; 1:46.00)

2:17.20 Vladimir Shuvalov, U.S.S.R., Tallin, Feb. 21, 1966
2:16.80 Alain Mosconi, France, Paris, July 13, 1967
2:16.30 Alain Mosconi, France, Marseille, July 20, 1967 (29.00; 1:03.50; 1:45.20)
2:13.50 Frank Wiegand, D.D.R., Leipzig, Nov. 6, 1967 (28.60; 1:03.00; 1:43.70)
2:13.50 Roland Matthes, D.D.R., Magdeburg, Aprl. 20, 1969
2:13.00 Vladimir Kravchenko, U.S.S.R., Novosibirsk, Apr. 15, 1970
2:12.80 Roland Matthes, D.D.R., Brandenburg, July 11, 1970
2:09.30 (*W.R.*) Gunnar Larsson, Sweden, Barcelona, Sept. 12, 1970 (28.00; 1:00.90; 1:39.50)
2:07.17 (*W.R.*) Gunnar Larsson, Sweden, Munich, Sept. 3, 1972 (28.00; 1:01.07; 1:38.07)

European Progressive Records List for 400 Metres I.M. (*Men*)
(*Long Course*)

5:12.90 (*W.R.*) Vladimir Stroujanov, U.S.S.R., Moscow, Oct. 20, 1957
5:08.80y (*W.R.*) Ian Black, Great Britain, Cardiff, June 6, 1959 (1:10.50; 2:34.50; 4:02.80)
5:06.90 Boris Nikitin, U.S.S.R., Moscow, Apr. 15, 1962 (1:08.00; 2:26.20; 3:55.20)
4:53.80 (*W.R.*) Gerhard Hetz, West Germany, Moscow, May 24, 1962 (1:04.70; 2:20.60; 3:48.30)
4:50.20 (*W.R.*) Gerhard Hetz, West Germany, Tokyo, Oct. 12, 1963 (1:03.70; 2:19.20; 3:44.00)
4:50.20 Andrei Dunaev, U.S.S.R., Moscow, July 12, 1966 (1:04.40; 2:18.00; 3:45.00)
4:47.90 Frank Wiegand, D.D.R., Utrecht, Aug. 22, 1966 (1:05.70; 2:16.90; 3:44.10)
4:47.20 Andrei Dunaev, U.S.S.R., Moscow, Aug. 1, 1967 (1:06.10; 2:20.00; 3:42.50)
4:45.30 (*W.R.*) Andrei Dunaev, U.S.S.R., Tallin, Apr. 3, 1968
4:44.00 Michael Holthaus, West Germany, Berlin West, Aug. 30, 1968
4:43.00 Hans Fassnacht, West Germany, Los Angeles, Aug. 2, 1969
4:42.50 Hans Fassancht, West Germany, Wurzburg, Aug. 24, 1969 (1:03.50; 2:15.80; 3:40.30)
4:41.80 (prelim) Gunnar Larsson, Sweden, Barcelona, Sept. 7, 1970

4:36.20 Gunnar Larsson, Sweden, Barcelona, Sept. 8, 1970 (1:04.30; 2:15.90; 3:36.10)

4:34.99 (prelim) Gunnar Larsson, Sweden, Munich, Aug. 30, 1972

4:31.98 Gunnar Larsson, Sweden, Munich, Aug. 30, 1972

4:31.11 Andras Hargitay, Hungary, Belgrade, Sept. 5, 1973 (1:00.31; 2:09.33; 3:29.32)

European Progressive Records List for 400 Metres I.M.
(Women) (Long Course)

5:49.10y Lenie De Nijs, Holland, Durban, Mar. 8–9, 1958

5:49.00 Heidi Pechstein, D.D.R., Leipzig, Apr. 16, 1961 (1:17.80; 2:49.00; 4:32.20)

5:40.90 (second) Marianne Heemskerk, Holland, Zwolle, Aug. 20, 1961

5:39.40y (second) Judit De Nijs, Holland, Blackpool, Aug. 26, 1961 (1:18.20; 2:43.40; 4:20.50)

5:36.00 Marianne Heemskerk, Holland, Rotterdam, Feb. 28, 1962 (1:11.90; 2:38.20; 4:19.60)

5:33.10 Adrie Lasterie, Holland, Den Haag, July 29, 1962 (1:15.50; 2:45.80; 4:21.80)

5:27.80 Adrie Lasterie, Holland, Leipzig, Aug. 25, 1962 (1:14.20; 2:40.50; 4:15.40)

5:26.80 (prelim) Veronika Holletz, D.D.R., Tokyo, Oct. 15, 1964 (1:13.60; 2:34.70; 4:11.20)

5:25.60 (fourth) Veronika Holletz, D.D.R., Tokyo, Oct. 17, 1964 (1:13.50; 2:36.80; 4:12.30)

5:25.00 Elizabeth Heukels, Holland, Utrecht, Aug. 27, 1966 (1:12.70; 2:39.50; 4:10.70)

5:22.60 Sabine Steinbach, D.D.R., Leipzig, Apr. 9, 1967

5:14.90 Sabine Steinbach, D.D.R., Tallin, Apr. 2, 1968

5:07.90 Evelyn Stolze, D.D.R., Barcelona, Sept. 6, 1970 (1:08.80; 2:28.00; 3:58.40)

5:06.96 (prelim) Evelyn Stolze, D.D.R., Munich, Aug. 31, 1972 (1:09.48; 2:28.28; 3:57.98)

5:03.99 (third) Novella Calligaris, Italy, Munich, Aug. 31, 1972 (1:09.64; 2:27.19; 3:57.63)

5:01.10 (W.R.) Angela Franke, D.D.R., Utrecht, Aug. 18–19, 1973

4:57.51 (W.R.) Gudrun Wegner, D.D.R., Belgrade, Sept. 6, 1973 (1:06.65; 2:23.98; 3:51.34)